Tukaram

The Ceaseless Song of Devotion

Mystics of the East Series

Tukaram

The Ceaseless Song of Devotion

Chandravati Rajwade

RADHA SOAMI SATSANG BEAS

Published by:
Sewa Singh, Secretary
Radha Soami Satsang Beas
Dera Baba Jaimal Singh
Punjab 143204, India

Third edition (revised) 2004

ISBN 81-8256-049-7

Printed in India by:

Galaxy Offset (India) Pvt Ltd, B-83, Naraina Phase - II
New Delhi - 110028

*This book is humbly dedicated
to all the four Masters
at whose lotus feet
I have had the good fortune of sitting.*

Make me small and humble, O Lord,
For only a tiny ant can pick up
Grains of sugar from sand.

Tukaram

Contents

Preface

THIS BOOK WAS FIRST PUBLISHED IN 1978 as part of a series on the lives and teachings of different Eastern mystics. Saint Tukaram, a poet-mystic from Maharashtra in India, was included in the series because his teachings contain truths that transcend all limitations of time, place and language, and coincide in their essence with the teachings of all the great spiritual teachers.

Tukaram's teachings, like those of other Maharashtrian saints, have been passed on in the form of *abhangs,* a style of devotional poetry particular to the Marathi language. The literal meaning of the word *abhang* is 'ceaseless' or 'unbroken'; it therefore seemed fitting to include the word 'ceaseless' in the title of this book. The Ceaseless Song also refers to the Shabd, the Word, the Name of God, the infinite energy by which this universe and all the heavens were created and through which the soul returns to its Creator.

Tukaram taught that the purpose of human life is to remember the Lord, who lives within each one of us and can be realized through a method Tukaram calls the "easy way". But we can only follow this way and merge in the Song that is ringing within us if we find a living teacher who has already gone where we wish to go, and who is therefore in a position to help us. Tukaram's poetry describes his own search for God and the bliss of surrender to the Lord and his Master, and offers advice to others treading the same path.

This book presents a summary of Tukaram's life and teachings as well as a sampling of his poems. Although we may find it of interest as history or even as literature, Tukaram's purpose in writing his poetry was to inspire and support those who wished to follow his teachings. Tuka was himself a model—he lived completely in accordance with his lofty teachings. When he found a Master who taught him the method of realizing the treasure within, he went against the orthodoxy and exhorted people to stop looking for the Lord in outer observances and to engage in meditation—the "business that will profit you". Tukaram's story is a story of devotion and detachment in the face of hardship, and unflinching faith in the Lord and his teacher. His poetry tells this story.

Tukaram's poems are given in this book in the order in which they appear in the Marathi collection to allow readers to browse from one poem to another and discover for themselves the breadth and depth of his work. For those who wish to find material on a particular topic, a subject index has been included. Explanations of technical, philosophical, mythological, Indian-language and other terms with unusual usage have been provided in a glossary. Sources for all quotations are given in the endnotes, with page citations and the first few words of each quotation provided for ease of reference. For those who are familiar with Tukaram's work in the original, an index of first lines of the poems in Marathi using roman script is appended.

In this third edition, additional information has been added to the 'Life and Teachings' section, and the poetry section has been expanded to give the reader a chance to more fully explore the treasure of Tukaram's teachings.

Sewa Singh
Secretary

Radha Soami Satsang Beas
January, 2004

PART ONE

Life and Teachings

Introduction

FROM THE THIRTEENTH CENTURY to the seventeenth century, the State of Maharashtra was blessed with a great many saints. Their forceful teachings urged people to live with determination, fearlessness, humility and compassion. They awakened the slumbering masses and inspired them to strive with faith and devotion towards God-realization. These saints of Maharashtra produced a vast treasure of mystic literature which continues to inspire people today, irrespective of their caste, creed, race or nationality.

During these four centuries the seeds of sainthood seemed to fall like manna from heaven and at least fifty saints were born in Maharashtra into various castes and social strata. Dnyaneshwar, Eknath and Ramdas were brahmins, Namdev was a tailor, Narhari a goldsmith, Gora a potter, Savata a gardener, Sena a barber, Chokha Mela a sweeper (an untouchable), Jami a maid servant and Joga an oil-press worker. Tukaram was a *kunbi* (peasant farmer) by caste and a trader by vocation. Each of these saints earned his or her own living. None was a burden on society unlike many of the priests and preachers of that time, who would often take advantage of people's blind faith.

This span of four centuries was a very special period in the history of the bhakti movement, not just in Maharashtra but also in other parts of India. This movement emphasized seeking God-realization by means of true devotion to God without expectation of any reward—in other words, by means of complete surrender. The saints taught and their teachings were written down in their local languages instead of in Sanskrit, the language of the scriptures.

As S.G. Tulpule says, "They gave to India the concept of democratic mysticism." The doors of these mystics and spiritual teachers were always open to all seekers, irrespective of their caste or social status. Whoever entered was welcomed as a brother—nay more, was honoured as a saint and was addressed as *sant* (saint). The mystics were noble souls, but they addressed their devotees *as sants,* not just out of humility but also because they saw in each devotee the capacity to become a saint. Even in the Adi Granth, the Gurus address their devotees as *santo* (O saints) or *sadho* (O holy men).

Pandharpur, a town 480 kilometres from the city of Mumbai (Bombay), became the centre of the bhakti movement in Maharashtra. There, the movement was popularly known as *bhagavat dharma,* which is defined as "a religious way of life based on devotion as the means for the realization of the identity of the Supreme Being and the individual soul".

In Pandharpur there is a temple dedicated to Vitthal. The *abhangs* (devotional poems) of the saints make it clear that "Vitthal" is just another name for God. Out of their deep love for the Lord, saints called him by many names, including Vitthal, Pandhari, Pandurang, Ram, Krishna and Hari.

The spiritual activities of the temple focused on *nam samkirtan* (spiritual discourses), *kirtan* (solo and group singing) and meditation. *Nam samkirtan,* as the name suggests, means praising the Name of God in discourses. The importance of remembering the Name of God and repeating it was stressed in the discourses. During kirtan, devotees sang songs of longing for divine union composed by these saints. These songs were not just pleasing to the ear but also pregnant with mystical thoughts. They emphasized finding balance and harmony between spiritual and worldly activities, which appealed to the people, especially as they were composed in their native tongue, Marathi. This set them apart from the Hindu scriptures which were written in Sanskrit and as such beyond the comprehension of the common people.

Prof. K.V. Belsare explains that Indian culture is basically an idealistic one, which believes in a spiritual reality that goes beyond the senses, yet most Indians also believe in keeping a harmonious balance between spiritual and worldly activities. Sense pleasures are not rejected but kept in their proper place. The following abhang by Tukaram illustrates this approach:

> Indulge not the body in sense pleasures,
> But do not inflict penance on it either,
> Nor take recourse in renunciation –
> By itself the body is neither good nor bad.
> Make haste, says Tuka, dedicate yourself
> To the Lord's Name.

The term 'saint' is used throughout this book in a special sense. A saint is a person who has reached the supreme height of self-realization. He sees God face to face and enjoys unalloyed divine bliss. He knows God so intimately that he himself becomes divine. His life is holy in all its aspects. He is master of himself and belongs to the Kingdom of God. He is a warrior—but a warrior of a particular kind. He has had to overcome tormenting conflicts between self-will and surrender to the will of God. A person reaches sainthood when he wins this battle. Then the light of God burns steadily in his heart.

Through inner knowledge, a saint understands the divine purpose at work not only within himself but throughout the entire universe. Realizing the presence of God both within and without, he is able to willingly cooperate with the divine purpose. As such he is able to face the ups and downs of life with sublime serenity. He remains unmoved by the calamities of worldly life because he sees the divine hand working behind every event. Holiness, fearlessness and love for all beings are the marks of a saintly life.

A saint derives great strength from his contact with God. He pours that strength into the hearts of those men and women who labour to find peace in life. Hence a saint is a constant source of inspiration and solace to the sorrow-ridden world. His benevolence knows no bounds. He is untouched by narrowness or meanness. He is a great soul in every sense. He is a wise man who carries the torch of knowledge to dispel the darkness of human ignorance. He leads people towards God with gentleness and tact.

Unfortunately, the contemporaries of a saint often treat him with contempt. The wicked generally persecute and torment him, but this neither affects his faith in God nor disturbs his inner peace. Though a saint outwardly resembles an ordinary human being, inwardly he is one with the Lord. A saint, in short, is God on earth.

Tukaram was a saint to whom all the above applied. Of all the Marathi-speaking saints who have left an indelible mark upon the culture and the people south of the River Narmada, Tukaram has been acclaimed as the greatest in terms of popular esteem. More than any other saint, his life and teachings, his personality and his compositions have penetrated deeply into the religious, cultural and social life of Maharashtra. Even today, some four hundred years later, his abhangs are sung with ardour and enthusiasm in many a Maharashtrian home.

Life Sketch

Early life

The year 1598 has been generally accepted as the most probable date of Tukaram's birth. He was born at Dehu near Pune (Poona) in the State of Maharashtra where his ancestral home still exists today.

Vishwambhar, a contemporary of Saint Namdev (1270–1350), is considered to be the earliest known ancestor of Tukaram. Tukaram's father was named Bolhoba and his mother Kankai. Bolhoba was a *mahajan* (village chieftain) and as such possessed a large piece of prime agricultural land. He supported his family with the earnings from his shop, where he sold grain and other farm produce from his own land. In those days, however, a grain seller was considered to be lowborn, and as such he was looked down upon by the learned priestly class.

Bolhoba was essentially a religious man, and although busy as a merchant farmer, he was also deeply devoted to the family deity known as Vitthal or Pandurang. In fact, his entire family was noted for their devotion to God. Tukaram inherited this legacy.

Tukaram had a normal childhood. Like other children of his age he took part in village games, some of which are described in his poems. As was the custom, his father arranged for him to be married at the age of thirteen. His wife, Rakhumai, was only eight years old. However, as she was asthmatic, Tukaram's father married him again the following year to a girl called Jijai, also known

7

as Avali.* Once married, Tukaram led a normal householder's life and helped his father in his business. The family enjoyed reasonable prosperity. They had a comfortable life with servants to help in the home and in cultivating their land. They also owned cattle that ploughed the fields and supplied them with milk.

Tukaram was respected and liked by all on account of his goodness, truthfulness, honesty in business dealings and kind nature. He could never believe that cunning and deceit could dwell in anyone's mind. He firmly believed that God fills the heart of every person.

Thus the upright and pious Tukaram passed his days free from want and worry. But his happiness and the well-being of his family did not last. They had to face a devastating famine which occurred around 1619, when he was just twenty-one years old. He suffered heavy losses in trade, losing his cattle and other wealth. He was reduced to poverty and was forced to borrow money for the maintenance of his family.

Soon the moneylenders started harassing him. The same society which had held him in high esteem started despising him. He could not look to his parents for support and guidance as he had lost them when he was only seventeen. He had no friends or relatives to depend upon as they too had left him when he was beset with problems. Food, once abundant in his home, became increasingly scarce and soon there was nothing left to eat. Tukaram's first wife, Rakhumai, and their son, Santu, eventually died of starvation.

With the loss of his parents, wife and son, and the loss of all means to support himself and his family, Tukaram became

---

* Although it was not common practice, parents at that time would sometimes arrange for a son to take a second wife, while still providing for the first wife, if the first wife had health problems.

miserable and despondent. He felt utterly alone. Everywhere he could find only darkness and disappointment. He laments:

> Deeply grieved am I with the sorrows of the world.
> My mother and my father are no more,
> The famine has destroyed all my property,
> And my prestige in society is lost.
> My wife has died for want of food,
> My business suffered a heavy loss.
> I am put to shame,
> I am consumed by sorrow.

Tukaram describes his state of mind in the following poignant words:

> I am harassed to the extreme from all sides –
> Whose shelter should I seek now?
> I cannot bear to know any more of worldly life;
> No one belongs to me.

Tukaram suffered mental trauma, resulting in his total disillusionment with the world. Even though circumstances conspired against him and deprived him of all security, this experience ultimately had a positive impact on him, for destiny had something better in store for him than to remain engrossed in worldly life. "Loss of health or wealth or sudden death of a loved one are shattering experiences which often help to awaken the slumbering self," observes Belsare. This was the case with Tukaram, who became increasingly introverted as a result of the adversities forced upon him.

His suffering made him poignantly aware of the futility of worldly pursuits and brought out his latent spiritual bent of mind. He realized that the pleasures of life were superficial and temporary. He saw that they only hid the face of disease, starvation, humiliation, disaster and death. He recognized that life goes with death, health with disease, youth with old age and pleasure with pain. In one of his poems he proclaims:

> The body and riches are a mirage,
> They are not true, they will decay and perish.
> Through calamities, the Lord has created in me
> Aversion to worldly life.

It dawned on Tukaram that genuine happiness was to be found only in the love of God. God alone is real and all else is deception, a game played by maya (illusion). His innermost feelings are expressed in this verse:

> There is no peace on this earth.
> Man is always engulfed in worldly affairs,
> Taking no thought of the Lord and spirituality.
> He is too engrossed in sense pleasures,
> Toiling night and day for his family.
> But they are never satisfied,
> And keep him from seeing the Lord.
> O man, this amounts to suicide.
> You make a grave mistake
> By neglecting the Lord.

There was a complete change in Tukaram's attitude to people and their affairs. He became a different person, transformed from within. So radical was this transformation that he came to see the loss of his parents, wife and son as not just an act of God but also a blessing in disguise. The following lines show the transformation that disaster wrought in Tukaram:

My wife is dead, she is freed from suffering –
The Lord has released me
From the maya of attachment.
O God, it is just you and me;
No one is left to come between us.
My child is dead, that too is good –
The Lord has freed me from all attachments.
Says Tuka: my mother has breathed her last –
The Lord has taken away all my anxieties.

The raging fire of worldly miseries burned away the very roots of his love and attachment for worldly affairs. The seed of devotion to God automatically took root in the scorched soil of his soul. Tukaram made a firm resolve to search for the real meaning of life. His sights were set on the ultimate reality and he resolutely set out to realize it within himself. He had no other desires left and became indifferent to worldly things. He says to himself:

Let me not desire anything, O Tuka;
Let me go away, discarding everything.

Search for a saint
Having turned his face towards God, Tukaram started studying holy books and the writings of past saints such as Namdev, Dnyaneshwar, Kabir and Eknath. He also saw the great importance

of keeping the company of living saints and listening to their teachings. He expresses in the following poem his earnest desire for the company of those who love God:

> Life's mission will be fulfilled on meeting saints.
> I long for them –
> Happy is the day when I meet them.

Tukaram never lost an opportunity of spending time with saints and true devotees. He declares:

> The sun, the lamp and the diamond
> Show things which are visible.
> But the saints show things which are invisible.
> Parents are the cause of birth,
> But saints are the cause of the cessation of birth.
> Go and be in the company of saints,
> Even if you are not invited.

In his poems he is full of praise for the saints, whose "words are like nectar" for the spiritually thirsty.

> If your heart merges in the heart of a saint
> Then you will have achieved everything.
> Otherwise the company of saints has been in vain,
> For you will be like a stone which sits in water
> All the time, but is quite unchanged within.

Tukaram asks the Lord to keep him at the feet of the saints lest he forget God's Name: "Even if he could not find God, he should at least be fortunate enough to live in the company of saints." Being with such saints is described by him as more sacred than going to places of pilgrimage.

Tukaram recognized that meditation is the key to God-realization. He pleads with the Lord, "I wish to do ceaseless repetition…With my body, mind and tongue I want to do only this…Let my mind be intoxicated with your Name." Being basically a lover of solitude, he liked the lonely hills of Bhambnath (Bhambgiri) and Bhandara near his home in Dehu. He would sit there in meditation for hours on end with intense longing to know the ultimate reality. He did not move his body even slightly when meditating, nor was he ever afraid, even though he was constantly assailed by reptiles, scorpions and tigers.[*] In order to stay awake he used to tie a cord to his hair and fasten the cord to a peg above him saying, "When my neck feels a jerk, my drowsiness will leave me."[†]

Initiation, spiritual practice and longing

Tukaram prayed fervently to the Lord to send him a Master to give him proper guidance on the spiritual path. He was quite confident that the Lord would commune with him in the silence of his soul. He confesses his helplessness to the Lord thus:

> I am weary even of my own family –
> What does it matter how the world treats me?
> Other than the Lord, I have no relatives or friends.

---

[*] This is reminiscent of a story about Valmiki, who wrote the well-known Hindu epic *Ramayana*. It is said that he sat for meditation for so long that an anthill *(valmik)* formed around him, and he was unaware of being covered with the ants.

[†] Baba Jaimal Singh Maharaj, the first Master of Radha Soami Satsang Beas, also did this to overcome sleep during meditation.

His love for the Lord was so strong that he said, "I crave neither heaven nor salvation; I want only your Name and ceaseless love for you."

It was during this period of intensive meditation and prayer that Tukaram's Guru, Babaji Raghavachaitanya, showered his grace and initiated him in 1619. This was the beginning of the truly spiritual phase of Tukaram's life.

After initiation, Tukaram spent most of his time on spiritual practice as taught by his Guru. He knew that he had to purify himself of all worldly dross by getting rid of the six mental foes, which he identified as lust, anger, greed, attachment, envy and ego. Nothing else would make him fit for the Lord's grace and his vision.

Tukaram had to struggle hard to eliminate all that was not divine. His *Gatha* (collection of abhangs) is full of entreaties to the Lord to remove the obstacles on his spiritual path and to bestow his grace on him so that he could do what he needed to do to attain God-realization.

Tukaram knew that the main cause of misery in this world is the feeling of separation between God and his creation, and that happiness lies in being able to see that God is present in everything and everybody. He asks:

> When will I be lucky enough to see
> Only the Lord in everything and everybody?
> Then there will be no limit to my happiness.
> I will no longer have weaknesses
> Like lust and anger;
> Instead my mind will be filled
> With forgiveness and mercy.
> Discrimination will be my strength,

As strong as a burning fire.
Who else but you, O Lord,
Can fulfil this desire of mine!

Our attachments to worldly objects are very strong and in order to get rid of them we have to develop attachment to the Lord. Spiritual success depends on true detachment from the world. When a devotee recognizes that only God is permanent, that everything else is transitory and that lasting happiness lies only with the Lord, then he develops detachment and turns towards God.

As the saying goes, two swords cannot occupy the same scabbard. The heart can belong either to God or to mammon. For life after life, we are weighed down by worldly attachments and do not know how to get rid of them. Tukaram was deeply aware of this predicament. He says:

Let my throat cry for you,
Let my eyes weep for you.
With attachment to you
Let me be detached from everything else.
Nothing else is sweeter than your love.

On the spiritual path, the only object of love should be the Lord. The devotee should always think of him alone, no one else. It is often said, perhaps in jest, that God is a jealous lover who will not tolerate even the slightest love for anybody or anything else in the heart of his devotee. Tukaram admonishes himself:

How often must I tell you
Not to get entangled with anything?

15

It only brings sadness.
Those who are detached
Get the happiness of the Lord's love.
Don't worry about slander or praise,
Happiness or misery.[*]

A cow may be grazing in the forest
But her mind lies with her calf.
The moment a fish is taken out of water,
It struggles and suffers.
O God, such is my love for you.

Once love for the Lord is created, we become so anxious to see the Lord that we experience misery along with the love, and this is not an easy thing. About his love for the Lord, Tukaram says, "As the lover is dear to the beloved, so is the Lord to me. As a greedy man wants more and more treasure, so do I want the Lord." His love for the Lord became so ardent that he wanted the Lord's form fixed in his eyes all the time, asking, "Who cares for heaven when I have your love?" He appeals to the Lord, "Give me only your Name and your love. I want nothing else."

Tukaram got immeasurable joy in loving the Lord and innocently teased the Lord by saying that he, as a devotee, is at an advantage compared to the Lord himself:

What does the lotus know of its fragrance?
Only the bumblebee can enjoy it.

---

[*] Note that when two or more different poems are quoted in succession, the change from one poem to the next one is shown by double spacing. Each poem is sourced in the endnotes.

How can you enjoy your Name?
Only we know the happiness of love.

Tukaram was aware that one's sins come in the way of God-realization. He says, "My sins stand between you and me." At the same time, he recognizes that it is impossible for a human being to get rid of his sins unless the Lord helps:

I am a sinner,
But it is your duty to save me.

I am a sinner, but I am your marked soul, says Tuka,
So it is your responsibility to take care of me.

Mind is a formidable foe for spiritual seekers. It employs many tricks to block their spiritual progress and lead them astray. Tukaram tells his mind not to "get entangled in the great trap of this worldly mirage. Death is coming towards you to devour you. When he descends upon you, nobody other than the Lord will be able to save you." Tukaram is very persistent. Again and again he implores the Lord:

What shall I do with this mind?
It has no wish to give up sensual pleasures.
O Lord, only you can come to my rescue –
I do not think anyone else can control it.
Not for a split second can it remain steady;
It wants to jump headlong
Into this dreadful ocean of existence.

People are social beings. We like to spend time in the company of fellow human beings in fruitless discussion, time which would be better used in remembrance of God. Tukaram imposed on himself an extreme severity in social relations. He says, "I do not want to mix with people or talk about this and that." He begs of the Lord, "Please ensure that I do not like people…O Lord, with your authority, see that I remain only at your feet."

A spiritual seeker should be humble. In order to be fit to see God, he should not have any trace of ego in him. Tukaram's humility and his faith in the Lord are beautifully depicted in these lines:

> I am the fallen one, I am the fallen one.
> Three times over I repeat:
> I am the fallen one.
> But with your power
> Lift me up and make me whole.
> My heart is not pure,
> My thoughts are not with you,
> I am full of sin and folly.
> No words can describe one such as me.

The dark night of the soul

In spite of his steadfast devotion and his rigorous spiritual discipline, Tukaram had to experience the dark night of the soul before he found God. This period of sadness, turmoil, confusion, doubt, distress and restlessness comes in the life of every devotee. During such a period, Tukaram pleads with God:

> I have no strength to do yogic exercises,
> Nor do I know any other spiritual practices.

Though my heart's desire is to meet you,
I have no energy to do meditation.
What shall I do?
I am pining to meet you,
O merciful One.
Whom else shall I go to and ask?

Tukaram felt that he must be lacking the courage and strength to reach God. He begins to doubt whether God would ever show himself to him:

My meditation is so weak
That I am worried
Whether you will make me your own,
Whether I will get your vision,
Whether you will talk to me or remember me.

He entreats God to give him the gift of intense concentration while doing meditation. "Let me concentrate like a young girl carrying jars of water on her head and singing as she walks home with her hands free."*

He started to sit in meditation for long periods in the wilderness of the hills. While desperately awaiting the Lord's vision he tells the Lord:

I do not want honour and riches,
For they bring misery.

---

* Village girls in India go to a river or a well to fetch water with five or six pitchers. After filling them with water, they place them on their heads one above the other and walk back to their houses, chatting, gossiping and singing but with their entire attention on the vessels so that they do not drop them. Tukaram is beseeching God to favour him with this type of one-pointed attention while he meditates.

> Come and meet me –
> I want only your vision.
> Knowledge is of no use
> And miraculous powers are equally useless.

But the Lord did not oblige him. He did not answer Tukaram's prayer. And so Tukaram becomes restless:

> I long to be united with you,
> But alas, my desire has not borne fruit,
> For the time is not yet ripe.
> My heart is in turmoil,
> Like corn grains in a heated pot,
> Tossed violently and turned into popcorn.
> My yearning is inconsolable.

Tukaram kept on praying and further intensified his meditation with unshaken faith in his Master and the Name imparted by him. "I never cared for the opinion of the majority," he says, "I only relied upon the instructions of my Master and fully believed in the power of the Name."

He did not care about his body and often went without food for days on end. On such occasions his wife Jijai, although she disapproved of his non-stop devotion for the Lord, would bring bread to the jungle and search for him so that he could have at least a little food to sustain himself. Later, when often there was not a grain of food in the house, Tukaram would declare himself to be a guest of the Lord. He was even prepared to sacrifice his life in search of the Lord.

Tukaram's only desire was to see the Lord. This longing is expressed in a number of his poems:

O my Lord, I cannot be patient any longer;
Soothe me with your vision.

I am dying to see your form,
I am as uneasy as a fish out of water.
Please let me know how I can obtain you.

As a chakor bird waits for the full moon
And a daughter waits
For an invitation from her parents, *
As a hungry child awaits its mother,
So am I eagerly waiting day and night
To see your beautiful face.

I am suffering so much in my desire to meet you
That not a wink of sleep do I get,
And tears flow continuously from my eyes.
Fulfil your promise and meet me, O Lord.

O breath of my life,
Please remove the curtain
And grant me your true vision.

While thus beseeching God, he also castigates him for not
listening to his prayers and giving him his vision:

Why don't you have pity on me, my Lord,
Though you dwell right in my heart?
O heartless God, devoid of all goodness,

---

* Traditionally in India, when a girl has gone to her husband's house after
marriage, she must wait for an invitation to visit her parents.

21

I am crying my throat hoarse.
Why does my mind not obtain peace?
Why do my senses still bother me?
Why are you still angry with me? asks Tuka.
Are my sins not yet destroyed?

At the same time Tukaram is aware that without the grace of God his search will not succeed:

My endeavours have come to naught.
I have pinned my hopes only on you
And I await your grace alone, O Lord.

The Lord listened to his petition and granted him glimpses of his grace. At last, Tukaram saw God's vision and bowed at his feet. He is ecstatic:

I see God's face
And the vision gives me infinite bliss.
My mind is attracted by it
And my hands cling to his feet.
As I look at him,
All my mental suffering vanishes
And my happiness grows.

But when the Lord's vision did not come to him again, his rapture evaporated and his jubilation vanished. He was in great agony. Like many before and after him, Tukaram found that the "pilgrimage to God is an ascent full of ups and downs—ups consisting of flashes of God's grace and downs consisting of depths of despair".

Then this storm of disappointment and repentance began to wane—neither happiness nor misery lasts forever. Tukaram's mind cleared and he slowly became calmer and started to find peace. With faith and determination he kept on trying to see the Lord's face. He prays:

> O my Lord, let my eyes be forever
> Fixed on your form.
> Your form is so sweet,
> Your Name is so sweet –
> Endow me with your love forever.
> Grant me the boon that
> You remain forever in my heart.
> I do not ask for anything else
> Because all happiness lies at your feet.

Dr S. D. Pendse commented that the words "forever" and "heart" have deep significance in this poem because what Tukaram wanted was not something external, such as an idol in a temple, but something subtle and permanent in his heart.

He wanted to see the Lord with his inner vision. His desire was to remain in the Lord's company all the time. He implores:

> Pray, heed my last prayer, my beloved Lord.
> Body, mind and speech I surrender at your feet.
> May the union of my soul with the supreme soul
> Be forever cherished by my heart, says Tuka.
> Pray, come and make your abode in me, my Lord.

The condition of Tukaram's mind was such that he felt no attraction to anything other than the Lord and his Name. He declares, "My tongue has gone crazy, every second it utters only your Name."

Tukaram intensified his meditation with unshaken faith in his Master and the Name imparted by him, saying, "In my mouth let there be only your Name and let my whole being be filled with love for you."

God-realization

Tukaram's fervent prayers and his agonized cries in the wilderness of Bhambgiri were heard by the Lord at last. The Lord revealed himself to Tukaram in his formless effulgence. The dark night of the soul ended and enlightenment came to him. The Lord appeared when nothing but the Lord meant anything to him. This ultimate realization brought him boundless joy. Duality vanished and Tukaram became one with the Lord. He speaks of the revelation of the Lord in the following poem:

> After fifteen days I saw the divinity face to face.
> Lord Vitthal came to me in his formless effulgence
> When I was meditating on the plateau of Bhambgiri,
> And my agitated mind was stilled in Parbrahm.
> When I started contemplating on the Lord,
> Reptiles, scorpions and tigers surrounded me
> And I was constantly assailed by them.
> But I merged into the Lord
> As camphor merges into fire, says Tuka.

And he cries out in ecstasy:

> I have merged fully into the incomparable One
> And thus attained eternal unity...

Now I am merged in the form
Which is forever pure.

The sun and its rays cannot be separated,
Such is my relationship with the Lord now.

By divine grace, Tukaram's love conquered the Lord and his soul rested forever at the Lord's feet. He merged into the Lord and the Lord was visible to him everywhere. Who then was the worshipper and who the object of worship? It was an ineffable spiritual experience, for Tukaram found himself constantly in the presence of the Lord.

Several of Tukaram's abhangs are overflowing with the joy and excitement of this communion and the ambrosia of divine union:

The lamp in my hand has dispelled all darkness.
Grief has turned into happiness
And now I see goodness in all created things.

A stream of immeasurable happiness is flowing;
This happiness cannot be described.

Tuka has merged in the Lord
And is absorbed in supreme bliss.

After becoming a *jivanmukta,* one free from the chains of karmas and thus from the cycle of birth and death, Tukaram contrasts his previous state with his present freedom:

I experienced my own death —
It was a festive occasion beyond compare.

25

Now my joy fills all the three worlds
And I rejoice in being a part of the universal soul.
Till now I was confined to this world alone;
Ego was the barrier separating me from the Lord.
Now that I am devoid of ego, my joy knows no bounds –
Gone forever is the mire of birth and death.

Tukaram speaks of the sublime joy of constantly hearing the divine Melody around him:

The supreme state of bliss
Soars up above and around me
Like a canopy, a great shield.
The heavens are thundering
With the reverberating Sound divine.
Tuka's Lord has installed him in His own Self.

In this state, Tukaram saw the Lord everywhere and found that nothing in this world had any attraction for him any longer. He proclaims, "God is the giver and God is the enjoyer. What else remains to be said? Whatever I see is filled with him. Everywhere I hear the divine music." Further, he declares, "The outer world has no attraction for one who is absorbed in the unstruck music."

Reflecting on his life, Tukaram saw that he had been led to God-realization by the company of saints, their satsangs, initiation by his Guru and his own efforts in meditation. Most important of all was God's grace. Tukaram attaches importance to individual efforts, but describes these efforts as secondary to the Lord's grace. He says that he found God only because God's grace came down upon him, not because of any merit of his own.

Tukaram was aware, however, of the great effort he had to make to obtain God-realization. He declares, "I did service to the Lord without looking around me and without wasting a moment." But he humbly acknowledges that without the grace of the Lord no worship is of any avail: "The Lord has placed the treasure in my hands without receiving any service from me. Only by great good fortune was I able to see the Lord."

All the saints who have experienced inner visions have done so only by practising meditation day and night. Action is what matters; mere words are of no use. A lazy person can never make spiritual progress. In our worldly life, we have to take action to achieve anything; just as much action is required in our spiritual life. Only a brave soul can face the persecution and criticism of this world and conquer his senses. It is a constant fight. This is what Tukaram did to attain God-realization: "The impossible is made possible by effort. So it is with regular meditation."

Tukaram's mission

After God-realization, the third phase of Tukaram's life began. Now he lived only for the benefit of humankind, to impart the message of the saints and to guide people to God-realization. People were drowning in misery, something he could not bear to see. He now had a new purpose—to save others:

> I have been smaller than an atom,
> But now I have merged into Him
> And expanded to the outer limits of space...
> Now I exist only for the benefit of others.
>
> God is my constant companion.
> Like the saints of old

I have come down to this earth
To pursue the path of Truth.
By ringing the bell of devotion
With the help of his Name,
I shall carry you safe
To the feet of the Lord.

Tukaram's discourses in colloquial Marathi appealed to many. Those who came to scoff at him stayed to listen to his discourses and became his disciples. He had a number of distinguished disciples, among whom the names of Santaji Teli and Gangaram Mavla are noteworthy, since they are the ones who recorded his divinely inspired verses as he recited them.

Tukaram helped to dispel the feelings of spiritual helplessness among the downtrodden. Through his tireless teaching, he succeeded in awakening a consciousness not only of the equality of all human beings but also of their fundamental right to worship the Lord and realize him within. Tukaram strove to make people less passive, more conscious of their obligations and more united in the Name of God.

He restored dignity to human life and gave self-respect to the common people, who were victims of the caste system. Tukaram managed to convince people of the omnipotence of the Lord and of his protection, which imbued them with a sense of security and fearlessness.

Tukaram's hurdles and his persecution
Tukaram had to face enormous difficulties, both at home and in public. This was true not only while he was seeking God-realization but also later when he began to give out his spiritual message. His wife Jijai was indignant and angry that he spent

his time in spiritual endeavours. She was hostile and embittered because he subjected her and their children to privation and poverty. She would abuse the Lord and nag Tukaram mercilessly for neglecting his family.

Tukaram patiently put up with her admonitions by repeating the word 'Pandurang', his favourite name for the Lord. In one of his lyrics he even thanks the Lord for this 'good fortune', saying that if he had been blessed with a loving wife, he would have been bound by her love.

To appreciate the difficulties encountered by Tukaram it is necessary to understand the social and religious structure of Hindu society at that time. The caste system was predominant and the brahmins (the priestly caste) considered it their special privilege to worship God and to teach others how to find him. Tukaram did not belong to this caste. The scriptures were strictly out of bounds for a common man like him.

But in pursuit of his mission of spreading spirituality among the masses, Tukaram was giving soul-stirring discourses. His reputation started spreading far and wide and people began to revere him as a saint. Like many saints, he had to suffer ill-treatment by those who feared or envied his magnetic appeal. Orthodox Hindus were enraged that a lower-caste man such as Tukaram appealed so deeply to so many. They accused him of heresy for explaining the scriptures and the saints' teachings to ordinary people. As a result, he was persecuted by them.

Tukaram composed a number of poems and hymns in Marathi. He gave spiritual discourses interspersed with the singing of these hymns. For a lower-caste man to do this was considered sacrilegious and blasphemous by the brahmins, as he was encroaching upon their domain. Dilip Chitre writes:

Tukaram's first offence was to write in Marathi. His second and infinitely worse offence was that he was born in a caste that had no right to high Brahminical religion or for that matter to any opinion on that religion. Tukaram's writing of poetry on religious themes was seen by Brahmins as an act of heresy and in defiance of the caste system itself.

It is said that Rameshwar Bhatt, a staunch believer in tradition and Hindu orthodoxy, was so incensed by Tukaram's fame that he complained to the local court that Tukaram was engaged in heretical activities. The court ordered that Tukaram's poems and hymns should be thrown into the River Indrayani. With a sorrow-stricken heart Tukaram obeyed the order. He was told mockingly that if he were a true devotee of God, his sunken manuscripts would be retrieved and restored to him by his God. Saints do not mind being criticized themselves but they cannot bear the criticism of God or their Master. Tukaram sat in meditation on the river bank for thirteen consecutive days. Ultimately the Lord came to the rescue of his beloved devotee, and it is said that the river restored the manuscripts to Tukaram undamaged.

For persecuting Tukaram, Rameshwar Bhatt is supposed to have suffered bodily afflictions which were alleviated only when he took refuge in Tukaram. He then became one of Tukaram's most devoted disciples, recognizing him as a saint of the highest order. The Lord has many ways of bringing his marked sheep to the feet of the Master!

In another account of the troubles Tukaram had to bear, the story of Mambaji Gosavi is told. Mambaji was a self-appointed religious leader and a professional preacher. As more and more people flocked to listen to Tukaram's discourses, Mambaji's earnings dwindled. He was jealous of Tukaram's popularity and bore a perpetual grudge against him. Mambaji lived near Tukaram and had made a garden around his house. Once a buffalo which belonged to Tukaram's wife Jijai forced its way into Mambaji's garden and ate up many plants. Mambaji was greatly annoyed and he seized the opportunity to beat Tukaram with thorny sticks. Tukaram accepted the beating and the pain calmly while repeating the Name of the Lord. Jijai is said to have picked out all the thorns from Tukaram's body while she cursed his God for spoiling her domestic life.

Despite his hatred of Tukaram, Mambaji used to attend Tukaram's discourses. When Mambaji's absence was noticed at his next discourse, Tukaram enquired about him. He was told that Mambaji was in great physical pain. Tukaram at once went to him, prostrated himself before him and asked Mambaji to forgive him. Then Tukaram massaged Mambaji's body for a while and the pain is said to have disappeared. Mambaji, touched by Tukaram's kindness and humility, felt deep remorse for his insolent behaviour and a great change came over him.

The story is also told of the ill-treatment Tukaram endured at the hands of the wife of Gangaram Mavla, one of his disciples. She was so angry with Tukaram for making her husband follow him that she poured scalding hot water on Tukaram. Tukaram bore the insult and the physical pain, patiently keeping his thoughts fixed in the Name of the Lord.

The troubles and tribulations he suffered did not deter Tukaram in the least from pursuing his mission and leading an intensive spiritual life until he died in 1650 at the age of 52. During his last days he kept saying, "I am going to my hometown and I bid farewell to all."

Though he did not live long, he had a large following. His disciples led a truly spiritual life, diligently devoting themselves to the spiritual practice which he had taught them.

Tukaram as a person

Tukaram was simple, honest and straightforward. He was humble and kind-hearted. His patience and forbearance were remarkable. He had no pride or ego and no attachment to any worldly objects. His humility was boundless. He prays to the Lord:

> Make me small and humble, O Lord,
> For only an ant can pick up
> Grains of sugar from sand,
> While the mighty elephant
> Has to suffer the prodding of the goad.

He was happy to use his body and anything he had for the good of others. He would fan those who were feeling hot, give food to the hungry, give medicines to the sick and help the elderly with their shopping.

Tukaram always felt pity when he saw weary travellers carrying loads of luggage on their heads. He would often offer help to them by carrying the load on his own head. He would direct them to a temple or to the village square, and if they could not get shelter there, he would take them to his home, give them food and shelter and even massage and anoint their tired feet. He would feed and give water to their cattle.

Once a farmer who was going away asked Tukaram to keep watch over his fields. Tukaram gladly agreed, but he was so absorbed in repetition of the Name of the Lord that he saw only the Lord in the numerous birds feasting on the crop. When the farmer returned and saw the damage, he was beside himself with rage and brought Tukaram to the *panchayat* (village counsel) in order to have him punished. Later, when the corn was weighed, it was found that the grain was ten times the usual amount.

Tukaram's detachment from worldly possessions was very clearly seen when the Maratha king, Shivaji, sent him a gift of gold coins, ornaments and expensive clothes so that he could live comfortably. But Tukaram returned everything saying, "To me, wealth is like cow's meat;* an ant and a rich man are the same."

It was only his attachment to the Lord which detached him from the body and material objects. In this connection Justin E. Abbot observes: "Tukaram's asceticism may be misunderstood. He became an ascetic not because he saw in asceticism a way to some spiritual advantage, but because God became so central in his thought that he lost all interest in his body. He became a *videhi,* one so absorbed in the thought of God that he had no time or thought or desire to supply bodily needs. He ate when food was given to him, he slept only when nature compelled it."

Although the ascetic life seemed ideal for himself, Tukaram advised others to lead a normal householder's life with honesty and truthfulness and to perform their duty in a spirit of worship and surrender to the Lord. As a matter of fact, Tukaram himself never became a recluse, nor did he forsake his family. As best he could, he carried out his obligations to his family and society.

However, he had no time for worldly wealth if it disturbed his peace of mind. His father used to be a moneylender and it is said that he left his sons many promissory notes. Tukaram felt that with these documents he would always be thinking about whether he would get back his money, so he decided to throw

---

* Cow's meat is taboo for Hindus.

his share into the river. This incident is reminiscent of Soami Ji Maharaj tearing up the promissory notes that he had inherited from his father.

Tukaram's only purpose of life was God-realization. He did not care for wealth and the comforts of life. He did not crave honour or glory. His conduct always reflected his compassion towards all living creatures and his forgiving nature.

Tukaram's poems

Nearly five thousand abhangs or poems by Tukaram have been consolidated into a volume known as *Gatha* which, in Marathi, means a collection of spiritual verses. His surging thoughts about the Lord, the saints, the Name and other spiritual matters left his lips in the form of abhangs. Whatever he experienced, from being an ordinary mortal to reaching true sainthood, is expressed in his abhangs. Accordingly, the *Gatha* reveals Tukaram in all phases of his life and in all aspects of his religious beliefs and spirituality. His interest in rural games in his childhood, his family life, his attitude towards the family business, his forgiving nature, his truthfulness and kindness, his humility, his study of traditional folklore, all are vividly depicted in these poems.

His poems describe clearly his desires, his ambitions, his weaknesses, his difficulties in meditation, his doubts, the ups and downs of love and devotion, his hopes and disappointments and his ultimate jubilation. By way of his poetry, he invites people to share in God's treasure and cross the ocean of existence and go beyond the cycle of birth and death. Tukaram's great sympathy for all people and their sufferings is poignantly depicted in his poems.

Tukaram did not go through any formal study of scriptures, yet his compositions are full of spiritual mysteries. The language of his lyrics in the original is of incomparable sweetness and is full of deep devotion to the Lord. It is highly poetic and yet disarmingly simple. Tukaram used refined as well as rustic similes that are vivid and rich in meaning. His words are powerful and easily understood by simple village folk. Tukaram himself describes his poems as having been composed by God:

> If you say that I am composing this poetry,
> Then know that it is not mine.
> I cannot do it,
> I speak the Lord's words, not my own.
> How can a common man like me
> Know this deep philosophy?
> I say only what the Lord makes me say.

Among his abhangs there are some which are known as *paikiche* (foot soldier) abhangs. These abhangs have a symbolic meaning. They emphasize the fact that devotees have to become like soldiers. A devotee must fight against his own mind and against the pull of the world. These abhangs talk of heroism, comparing worldly soldiers with spiritual soldiers. Soami Ji Maharaj says the same in the *Sar Bachan*—that only a person with the tenacity and perseverance of a soldier can become a saint *(sant sipahi)*.

It is the inner change which is most important. Tukaram says that until there is inner change, any outward greatness is empty. Tukaram's evolution from *bhakta* (devotee) to mystic is clearly seen in his poems.

Tukaram will forever remain a pillar of light, a beacon of hope, a perennial fountain of inspiration on account of all that he said and did. His poems are a great legacy to humankind.

Tukaram's Teachings

ALTHOUGH THE POEMS IN PART TWO of this book will show Tukaram's teachings in some detail, it may be useful to discuss them briefly here to give an overall view of his message. The teachings of Tukaram are no different from those of other saints of the highest order. He declares that he draws them from the same mine of Truth which has been in existence since time began. These teachings have since gathered dust and their true meaning has been obscured by the passage of time. So he has come to explain them anew.

Because of his spiritual attainments, he is fully qualified to do this. He himself says that he is a resident of the Lord's abode who has come down for the benefit of the people of his time.

The significance of human birth

Like all saints, Tukaram says that our soul is part of the supreme soul, the omnipresent Lord, and that there is no difference between the two. The oneness of the individual soul and the supreme soul is revealed in the following poem:

> Cream, curd and butter all come from the same milk,
> Various ornaments are made from the same gold,
> Different pots are fashioned from the same clay.
> Just so, the Lord takes many forms,
> But in them all is the one soul.

The soul, having trapped itself in maya, collects good and bad karmas and continues to go round in the cycle of birth and death. It runs after the mirage of worldly happiness, never finding any lasting peace. Tukaram describes the plight of the soul in the following lines:

> The soul was in truth free,
> But it chose to be bound
> By getting entangled in 'me' and 'mine'.
> It tires itself out running after a mirage
> Like a deer in pursuit of water.

Like all saints, Tukaram says that only after many lives and with much good karma does one obtain a human life. This life should be used for devotion to the Lord in order to attain liberation from the cycle of birth and death and to return to him. He tells the Lord about himself in one of his poems:

> After many years I got this fortune of your devotion.
> Now I'll sacrifice my life for it
> And burn away this worldly life.
> I worry that once this human life is over
> I may not get another one.

Tukaram, like other saints, talks about the human body as "the temple of the living God" where the Lord is to be sought and realized. He declares that even the gods crave a human body so that they can merge with the Lord and have eternal happiness. A life of devotion to the Lord can only be lived in the human body.

Tukaram is against procrastination in the matter of devotion. He exhorts:

When you get a human birth
Repeat the Lord's Name and obtain happiness.
Like a thief, the Lord of Death is following you
And counting your days.
So hurry up, don't delay;
The time of death is not in our hands.

Outer display, external religious practices, rituals and ceremonies

It is said by Tukaram and other saints that God can be realized only in the human form. The question then arises—how to find him? Generally, people are ignorant of how to realize God. They are misled by charlatans, or by ignorant priests, or by their own traditional beliefs. They go to man-made places of worship to engage in rites and rituals. They go on pilgrimages, or to mountains or forests in search of God. Tukaram asks them:

What have you gained by pilgrimages to holy places?
You have merely washed the exterior of your body.
In what way has your mind been purified
That such visits may be considered to be of any merit?
So long as there is no peace, forgiveness and mercy within,
What are you bragging about? asks Tuka.

Tukaram explains that we find only water and stones in places of pilgrimage, whereas God is immanent in saints. To attain salvation it is not necessary to go to Varanasi* or to any such place.

---

* **Varanasi:** Indian city and place of pilgrimage, formerly known as Benaras or Banaras. Many Hindus believe that if they die in Varanasi they will attain salvation.

It is enough to behold a saint. Countless sins are destroyed by the darshan of a saint.

Tukaram denounces empty display, whether it be intellectual showing off, sitting in yoga postures or subjecting oneself to penances and austerities. None of these leads to knowledge of the Lord.

It is well known that early in his spiritual quest Tukaram worshipped his family deity Vitthal. Later, with his Guru's benediction and practice of Nam, he realized the Lord within himself and the name Vitthal became identified with the Supreme Being. Although Tukaram has dedicated a large number of poems to Vitthal it should be understood that Vitthal, Pandurang, Keshav, Hari, Narayan and Ram are simply some of the names he has given to the Supreme Lord. He describes the Lord as follows:

> O Lord, you are supreme bliss incarnate,
> Free from attributes, invisible,
> Inconceivable, infinite and eternal.
> You willingly take on many names and forms
> Depending on our level of devotion.

Initiation by a true Master

If outer search is useless, then what will lead us to God? Tukaram counsels that initiation by a true Master (Satguru) is essential. At the time of initiation the Master gives the disciple the gift of Nam and imparts the correct technique of meditation. He connects the disciple's soul with the divine Sound within and helps him on the inward journey, thus enabling the disciple to attain his goal. Tukaram says:

> The Shabd is truly the essence of everything…
> It is the greatest gift which can be given.

> Knowledge of the Ultimate can be obtained
> Only through the Satguru.

He therefore fervently prayed to the Lord to send him a Master to guide him on the spiritual journey back home. When the Lord finally reveals himself, Tukaram humbly expresses his gratitude and indebtedness to his Master:

> My Master has blessed me
> And now I live in the rhythm
> Of the divine Melody.

> By the grace of my Satguru,
> The Light has been lit within me.

Like other saints, Tukaram sees the Master not just as someone who is one with the Lord, but as the Lord himself. He declares, "The Lord has met me in the form of my Master." He therefore exhorts:

> Lest this human birth be wasted,
> Pray serve at the feet of the Satguru.

Qualifications and obligations of seekers

Spiritual seekers should be sincere and devoted; their sole objective should be God-realization. They should have full faith in the Master and his teachings. They should be prepared to surrender themselves completely and sacrifice everything for the love of the Master and the Lord. Tukaram says:

> If you love your Master with your whole heart
> You have achieved everything.
> Otherwise his company won't help you.
> Water and stone live together
> Yet the pebble remains dry within.
>
> As the moth loves the flame
> And burns itself in it,
> This is how to love the Lord.

Seekers may be literate or illiterate, men or women, married or unmarried. They may be from any social background, but they should be honest and truthful. They should not be a burden on anybody. They may be householders; they need not be celibates or ascetics. Tukaram himself was not an ascetic; he was a trader and householder. Seekers should also be vegetarian and abstain from alcohol. They should not desire the wealth of others. They should not concern themselves with members of the opposite sex outside their own families. But all of this is not enough. Tukaram says:

> It is only a person with past merits
> Who is drawn to the company of the saints.

A true Master

Tukaram emphasizes the point that we cannot achieve liberation from the cycle of birth and death without a true Master. Only such a Master can help us to practise meditation, contact the Shabd

41

and thus attain liberation in this life itself. Tukaram cautions that utmost care should be taken by a seeker when accepting someone as his Master, since true saints are rare in this world, but there are many frauds who pose as true saints. He says, "If an exhausted man goes to another exhausted man, both of them will perish."

He deplores those who pose as sadhus by donning ochre-coloured robes, going about with matted hair and begging for alms from door to door. He condemns such a life, which makes one a parasite on society. He warns against such sham sadhus and speaks out in no uncertain terms against hypocrites and fakes. He observes:

> Clothes do not make someone a saint,
> A poet is not necessarily a saint,
> Relatives of a saint are not saints.
> Reading scriptures, singing and making music
> Or going on pilgrimages
> Does not make anyone a saint.
> As long as a 'saint' does not forget his body
> He is a man of the world.

Then who is a true saint? Tukaram answers:

> A saint is one whose attachment is only to the Lord.
> His body, worldly wealth and honour
> Are as inconsequential to him as a blade of grass.
> He never misses meditation.
>
> He sees God everywhere.
>
> A saint's heart is like butter,
> Soft both inside and out.

He holds close to his heart
Those with no other support…
He is the very image of the Lord himself.

Saints come into this world
Only for the benefit of human beings.
For this, they endure bodily hardships –
Kindness is their asset.
Having no concern for themselves,
Saints are happy in the happiness of others
And nectar flows from their tongues.

A true saint comes with the inexhaustible treasury of God's
Name and gives from it freely to those who sincerely pray for it.
He teaches seekers the technique of meditation. When a seeker
meets a saint, he immediately sees the saint's majesty and gran-
deur, and that is more fascinating than anything that he heard
about the saint from others. Tukaram says of himself:

The Lord has sent me to this world
As bearer of his Name.

What do I know of deep philosophy?
I am his slave; his stamp is on me.

In a moment of ecstasy he issues an open invitation:

I have opened the treasure trove of the Lord's Name
With the measure of plenty in my hand.
Now there is a superabundance of the Lord's Name
Where there was once a shortage.

A time of plenty has come for the Name,
The famine is at an end.
Come, both young and old,
And enjoy these riches to your heart's content.

The Lord's Name or Nam

What is this 'Name' of the Lord which Tukaram and other saints talk about? The true Name of the Lord has been referred to by Tukaram and other saints as the Word, Logos, Nam, Shabd, Sound, Kalma, Tao, unstruck music, sound current, creative power of God and by many other terms. Tukaram says, "The Word is God; let us honour and worship the Word." He further says, "The unstruck music reverberates in all beings."

It is often thought that this Name is just a written or spoken word (or group of words), perhaps taken from scriptures, or perhaps passed on orally from guru to disciple, but this is not completely correct. The Name functions at two levels: at the human level it does function as the names given at initiation by a true Master, but the purpose of these names is to lead to concentration so the real Name can be realized. This unutterable Name functions at God's level as the divine melody, the Word, the Shabd. It emanates from the Lord and is experienced through soul consciousness. While repetition of the names given at initiation by a true Master can lead to the higher Name, this higher Name is quite unlike any of the names which we give to God; all such names are descriptive or attributive names. When Tukaram and other saints talk about the Name, they are generally referring to its Shabd aspect, to the power that created, pervades and sustains the entire creation. Only the true Name has the highest spiritual energy. It alone can lead the soul back to the Lord. Tukaram says:

With the Name
The wheel of births and deaths
Comes to an end.
This is the only way to happiness.
Put your trust in it,
Partake of this nectar.

If one is attached to the Name of the Lord
The mesh of illusion is cut asunder
And the ocean of existence evaporates.

The power of the Name is manifested in the form of sound and light. Tukaram refers to the sound and light of Nam in a number of his poems. The sound pulls the soul upward and the light illuminates the path. Sound and light are two aspects of the same power, the Word. Tukaram says of his experience:

Sitting at the Lord's feet, Tukaram is immersed
In a surging wave of divine Sound.

The Lord has taken up residence in me,
And the unquenchable flame shines there.

In another verse he talks about the potency of the Name thus:

What could not be understood in any other way
Can be grasped by uttering the Lord's Name.
What was invisible before
Will become visible by uttering the Name.
What was unutterable before
Will find expression on repeating the Name.

45

And the One who could not be found before
Will himself come to meet you on repeating the Name.

He summarizes the importance of Nam in Kaliyug (the Iron Age) thus: "In Kaliyug salvation is obtained only through the Lord's Name."

Meditation

A true Master not only bestows the gift of Nam on sincere seekers but also teaches them the technique of meditation. Meditation has three aspects or stages. First is simran, repeating the names given by the Master while concentrating one's attention at the midpoint between the eyebrows. Second is dhyan, contemplating on the form of the Master within. Third is bhajan, listening to the inner Sound. Correct meditation results in seeing the Master's form within and hearing the divine Sound. The Sound pulls the soul upward and the light associated with it shows the way to reach the realm of God. The Master's form guides the devotee on the spiritual journey.

It is difficult to endure the rigours of meditation unless one is truly courageous, dedicated to the cause and determined to achieve his objective. Tukaram says:

You will not be called valiant
If you are not able to face the rigours of meditation.
A diamond will shine in all its brilliance
Only after it endures the strokes of a hammer.

He also says that anything can be achieved with practice, effort and determination. A root manages to find a way through hard rocks; a rope can cut big stones; one can digest poison by consuming it in small doses. Likewise, God can be reached by regularity in meditation.

We need to have faith: "When you depend on him, the Lord will not disappoint you. But your efforts must match the efforts which you make for procuring earthly gains."

Simran

As long as one's attention is spread out in the world through the nine outlets of the body, one cannot hear the divine Sound and see the unquenchable flame within. When a devotee withdraws his attention from the nine outlets, concentrates it between the two eyebrows and repeats the Lord's Name as instructed by his Master, then his inner eye will open and he will experience sound and light. In Tukaram's words:

> The sun rises in the midst of darkness –
> Pierce through your third eye and see the brightness.
> Unless you concentrate at the third eye
> You will not see the bright sun within,
> Nor will you know yourself.

This is the only way to obtain God-realization. Remembering the Lord by ceaseless simran is the supreme prayer:

> One who repeats the Lord's Name with every morsel
> Gets the merit of fasting, even though he eats.
> One who repeats the Lord's Name while doing daily work
> Always has the bliss of meditation within him.
> One who repeats the Lord's Name while walking
> Gets the merit of *yagna* (sacrifice) at every step.
> Blessed is such a body,

> It has no need of pilgrimages and vows.
> One who repeats the Lord's Name
> Both in enjoyment and sacrifice of worldly pleasures
> Is not bound by his actions.
> One who thus repeats the Lord's Name ceaselessly
> Is liberated during this very lifetime!

Simran will enable the disciple to withdraw his consciousness to the eye centre, listen to the sound and see the light within, follow the inner spiritual path and come in contact with the Lord—the very aim of meditation. Ultimately, Tukaram says, "by repetition man becomes God."

Dhyan and darshan

As mentioned earlier, contemplation on the form of the Master is known as dhyan. If a devotee contemplates on the form of his Master, then ultimately the Master's inner, true form will appear within to guide him in his spiritual journey. This is darshan of the Master within. Without the Master's help within, it is impossible to realize God or even make any progress in the journey. Tukaram says:

> Inner contemplation is the real worship.
> Know this to be the secret, if you wish to know.

> My happiness knows no bounds
> When I see the Master's form within.

> An intense longing for you forever resides in my heart.
> I have seen your form once

And I am now unable to forget it.
My worldly affairs have ended
Because my attention is ceaselessly fixed on you.
My inner vision is now opened, says Tuka,
And you have revealed yourself to me within.

Bhajan

By constant repetition of the Lord's Name, a disciple experiences within himself the inner form of his Master and the inner sound and light. The act of listening to the Sound is known as bhajan. Tukaram calls it 'kirtan'. He says that it is this power of the Lord's Name that leads to the union of the soul with the Source, that is, the Lord. He counsels, "In Kaliyug, listen to the Sound. You will be able to meet the Lord." Tukaram declares:

When I become the Lord's slave
In thought, word and deed,
I hear the sound of cymbals *(tal)* and drum *(mridang)*.
When one is entranced by inner music,
All ill will is destroyed…
This ecstasy cannot be experienced
By Brahma and other gods.

The inner light, which was veiled,
Shone forth in resplendence…
The joy of seeing it
Cannot be compared to anything in the world.

The unquenchable flame shines within me
Since the Lord has taken up residence.

Dying while living

As already observed, it is through the practice of the Name that the consciousness pervading every particle of the body is withdrawn to the eye centre. This withdrawal enables a devotee to have spiritual experiences. Like Kabir, Dadu, Paltu, Namdev and other saints, Tukaram describes the process of vacating the body and reaching the eye centre as dying while living: "I have died to live." Saints say 'dying while living' because on completion of this process, the devotee has no feeling in any part of the body, yet the soul does not leave the body permanently, but returns to it after the meditation period is over. It is only by thus vacating the body that the soul can journey homeward with the help of the Sound and Light:

> Once my body was vacated,
> The Lord was enthroned within me.
> The care of my entire being
> Rests fully with him.
> Because of the death of my ego
> The Lord has taken up residence in me
> And the unquenchable flame shines there.

The mind

If God is not far away but resides within the human body, why is it so difficult to realize him? The most powerful obstacles on the spiritual path are mind and maya. In particular, to make spiritual progress we all have to struggle with negative emotions—lust, anger, greed, attachment, envy and ego. Reference has been made earlier to these forces, but they are discussed here again mainly with a view to focusing on the techniques taught to overcome them.

The mind is a strong force. As S.G. Tulpule says, "The first obstacle on the path of anyone who tries silent contemplation is the upspringing of varying mental impulses which invalidate the one-pointedness of yogic endeavour."

The mind is deeply attached to the objects and pleasures of the world. It runs after the illusory attractions of the world. It is fickle by nature and runs after worldly happiness. In the words of Tukaram, "Worldly happiness is like a mirage; it is never true."

The mind never recognizes the transitory nature of worldly happiness and so it keeps chasing worldly pleasure. It always wants one thing or another, so it never finds any lasting peace. Actions performed under the sway of the mind strengthen the seeker's attachment to the world. In accordance with karmic law we take birth again and again in various species in this world depending on the nature of our actions—both good and bad. Tukaram says that even our thoughts produce karmas:

> Merits and demerits
> Do not depend only on outer actions,
> But also on the thinking of the mind.

What is the solution? How can we point our mind in the right direction? The mind is a very bad master but a very good servant. The solution lies in slowly making it our servant by befriending it and giving it something better, higher, nobler and more interesting to pursue than worldly pleasures. In other words, we must provide the mind with something so attractive that it will lose interest in everything else.

Tukaram, like other saints, says that when it finds Nam or Shabd or divine Nectar, the mind will be satisfied once and for all. This is the only effective antidote for the waywardness, cravings and ills of the mind. The shackles of our karmas can be removed only by immersing our mind in Nam:

> Fix the mind on God,
> Do not allow it to wander,
> Avoid all laziness and sleep
> And embrace the Lord.
>
> Keep your mind in one place
> And get merged in the Lord's feet.

By practising Nam persistently as taught by the Master, the devotee can get the mind to cooperate, transcend the karmic law and attain God-realization.

Negative emotions

The mind's basic problem is that it mistakes the illusory for the real. In addition to this general problem, the mind presents us with a number of particular obstacles to overcome, which have already been referred to as "negative emotions": lust, anger, greed, attachment, envy and ego. The seeker must wage a constant battle against them to reach God.

> Control the senses and forgive others…
> Then only will you get the Lord.
> No crop can be obtained without working hard for it,
> So you have to go through trouble
> To control the mind and obtain God-realization.

In order to prevent the mind from having lustful fantasies he advises us "not to talk to a woman when alone." He prays:

O God, do not give me the company of other women.
Because of them I do not remember God,
Nor do my bhajan.
This mind cannot be controlled...
Beauty leads to misery.

According to Tukaram and all saints, the way to remove worry and misery is to have fewer wants and be unaffected by the ups and downs of life:

After all, how much does a person require!
Every day he needs a kilo of food
And six feet of space to sleep on.
All the rest is unnecessary.
So why forget the Lord
By getting attracted to other things
And thirsting for them?

One should live in this world
Uncontaminated by it,
As a lotus leaf lives in water
Uncontaminated by its drops.
Praise and censure must fall off his ears
As if he were absorbed within
In a state of ecstasy.
One should see the world
And yet it is to be taken as a dream.

We can only do this when we rid ourselves of the egotism which is at the root of all these emotions. Tukaram says: "One who has purged himself of ego is like a wish-granting gem...His mind is as clear as crystal."

The negative emotions attack the seeker and lure him away from the spiritual path. Tukaram advises us to attack these foes with the weapon of the Lord's Name. By doing so, we can replace lust with continence, anger with tolerance and forgiveness, greed and envy with contentment, attachment with discrimination and detachment, and ego with humility. We should surrender to God's will and use the weapon of repetition. This weapon costs nothing. It is God's gift:

> Due to the Lord's Name, I have become fortunate.
> My lust, anger and greed have melted
> And everywhere there is happiness.
>
> I have discarded for good all thoughts of
> Family name, good breeding and my appearance.
> I have offered my body to the Lord,
> To whom it really belongs.
> Now the ego has automatically been reduced to ashes,
> And by the grace of my Satguru
> The light has been lit within.

Worry, laziness, sleep and overeating

The other obstacles that Tukaram refers to are worry, laziness, sleep and overeating. As regards worry he says, "In life there is sometimes happiness, sometimes misery. Do not think of them too much. Don't let them affect you." He counsels, "Face whatever comes in life and don't blame the Lord. Then he will take care of you." We should give up all our worries and put our entire trust in the Lord:

> In the bosom of the stone there is a frog –
> Who feeds this frog but God!

The birds and serpents do not lay aside anything –
Who finds food for them but God!
When you put all your burden on God,
He, the Ocean of Compassion, will not neglect you.

Tukaram deprecates laziness, overeating and sleep as they are
not conducive to spiritual progress:

With laziness and sleep nothing can be achieved.
Laziness is a big enemy –
It even destroys our worldly life.
How then can it lead to God-realization?
One has to conquer it.
One way is to eat less.

He exhorts, "Do not sleep much, eat less…[thus] one gets
the Lord's grace and attains God-realization." Our food should
be simple. A heavy meal makes one lazy and lethargic. Tukaram
asks:

What shall I do with more sweets?
They will only take care of the body,
Which in any case is filled with disease.
Even dry bread
Will be as good as milk, sugar and butter
If it helps me to repeat the Name of the Lord.

Ethical conduct

Like other saints, Tukaram declares that the practice of Nam
bhakti and devotion to the Lord go hand in hand with ethical
and moral conduct, self-discipline and purification. He advocates

speaking the truth, living within one's means, abstaining from criticizing others, correct social and sexual behaviour, eating a vegetarian diet, abstaining from alcoholic drinks and not killing God's creatures. These are essential prerequisites for God-realization.

Tukaram asks: if you do not desire others' money, if you do not slander others and if you always treat other women as if they were your mother or sister, what do you lose? Why not believe what saints say? What effort is needed to speak the truth? Do only these things, he advises, and no other effort is needed to attach yourself to God.

Tukaram further talks about slanderers thus:

> We are obliged to these washermen
> For washing away our faults.
> By the soap of their words they take away our dirt
> Without charging us anything for it.
> They are coolies who work for nothing
> And take up our burden for us.
> They carry us to the other side of the ocean of life,
> While they themselves go to hell.

He deprecates meat eating and warns:

> The Lord is within every being –
> Don't they understand that he lives in animals too?
> When they can see these creatures
> Screaming in agony,
> How can the hands of these heartless ones
> Go towards their throats?

Such vile ones will have to suffer, says Tuka –
They will be hurled into the fires of hell.

The sole purpose of observing all the purificatory disciplines
is to free ourselves from any harmful impulses and keep us in such
a state of mind that we are able to meditate with devotion. Seekers
have to undergo all the rigours of a stern discipline. Tukaram says:

God-realization is not a joke;
To get it one must give up his life.
This life is like a seed which must be destroyed
So that corn can grow and be harvested.

Satsang and the company of devotees

Tukaram extols the benefit of attending satsang—keeping the
company of saints and their devotees. This helps to increase our
faith in the Master and his teachings and nurtures our love and
devotion for God. Tukaram stresses the importance of attending satsang when he says, "The Lord is present at satsang."

Satsang is compared to a stream of water in which a stone is
lying. Even if the stone does not melt, it is at least sheltered from
the heat. Satsang is also compared to a hedge built around a crop
to protect it from wild animals (bad company and our own weaknesses).

The company of saints purifies the seeker and elevates him.
Tukaram says, "The fires of the three attributes* can be extinguished only by the company of saints." He further says that the
saints "come into this world only to liberate humankind" and that

---

* **three attributes:** the three gunas—harmony, action and inertia. They are the
basic qualities of primordial matter out of which all creation proceeds.

their "words are like nectar" for the spiritually thirsty. Association with such saints is described by him as more sacred than any holy place of pilgrimage. While he praises the company of saints, he advises seekers to eschew evil company.

Summary of Tukaram's teachings

The sum and substance of Tukaram's teachings is that God is not a matter of speculation or assumption but a subject of perception and realization. The aim of human life is to work to find God and to know him. Only a true Master can enable us to achieve this objective. A spiritual aspirant should therefore first find a true Master and, after initiation by such a Master, he should follow the advice of that Master and fully imbibe his teachings. He should attend spiritual discourses and keep the company of sincere devotees of the Lord in order to live in an atmosphere conducive to spiritual practice. He should avoid the company of worldly people and live a pure and disciplined life so as to conquer the mind and master his own weaknesses. Then he will be able to gather his scattered attention at one point and meditate wholeheartedly. Meditation and devotion will lead him to God-realization.

PART TWO

Selected Verses

The Lord's Blessings

Oh, all you marked souls,
Come and share the Lord's prasad.*
Even Brahma and the other gods cannot obtain it,†
So appreciate its value and don't turn away from it.
The vessel is overflowing with this food,
It is the birthright of all.
The all-powerful Giver is right here
And he fulfils everyone's desires.
However much one tastes this nectar,
It never palls – one wants it more and more.
This food is served by the goddess of wealth,‡
Who assists the Lord in preparing it, says Tuka.

devaachya prasaade kara re bhojan, Gatha 40

---

* **prasad (prashad):** blessed food, a blessing, grace, generally used to refer to something blessed by the Master. Here prasad refers to the gift of initiation into the Name by the Master.
† Only in a human birth can one be initiated by a Master.
‡ **goddess of wealth:** the goddess Lakshmi. Her serving us indicates that all the gods and goddesses serve one who has a Master.

Keep Awake for Meditation

O mind, why don't you keep awake
For the Lord's meditation?
How can you ever make up for the time
Which you have wasted on your family?
Those you are entangled with
Will forsake you in the end.
So think now about God-realization –
That alone will help you, says Tuka.

harichya jaagrana, Gatha 42

Why Should I Worry?

I have given up all desires
And become indifferent to this world –
Now I have no fear of death.
Whether I shall lie low or sit high upon a horse
Is for you to decide, O Lord.
Why should I worry about it?
I have gone beyond honour and dishonour,
Happiness and misery,
And my mind is free from all cares, says Tuka.

aamhi tari aas, Gatha 47

Indifferent to Praise and Slander

Whether someone slanders me or praises me,
I am indifferent to both.
Whatever I have to face in life
Comes to me as a result of my own actions
And I will accept it all with equanimity.
Whatever happens is for our own good.
Since we have surrendered ourselves to the Lord,
He alone will face whatever comes to us, says Tuka.

nindi koni maari, Gatha 48

A Perfect Devotee

One who has purged himself of ego
Is like a wish-granting gem.
He slanders nobody, hurts nobody,
Thinks ill of nobody –
His mind is as clear as crystal.
He need not go to holy places
For he is the holiest place of all.
The world comes to him,
And the sight of him gives deliverance.
Docs one whose mind is pure
Need beads or any outward adornments?
He sings forever in praise of the Lord
So that his mind is filled with happiness.
He has given his body, mind and wealth
To the Lord and has no desires left.
Such a one is more precious
Than the philosopher's stone, says Tuka.
How can his greatness be described?

sakal chintaamani sharir, Gatha 53

Will You Lose Anything?

If you think of other women as your mother,
Will you lose any treasure?
If you do not slander others or desire their wealth,
Will you lose anything?
If wherever you are sitting you repeat the Lord's Name,
Will you need to toil hard for it?
Why not believe what saints say?
Tell me what you will lose!
What effort is needed to speak the truth –
Do you lose anything by it?
Do only these things, says Tuka.
No other efforts are needed to attach yourself to God.

paraaviya naari maaulisamaan, Gatha 61

A Contented Person Is the Richest

If your mind never feels contented,
Then even gold is no better than poison.
Whatever you desire too much,
Know that it will harm you.
What can I tell you?
You should know full well
That when your mind is in turmoil
Even sandalwood will burn the body,*
Not cool it, says Tuka.
Whatever remedies you may try,
Such a mind will always remain miserable.

chitta samaadhaane, Gatha 63

Empty Talk

If there are no tears in the eyes
When remembering the Lord,
And no ardent desire in the heart to meet him,
Then all talk about the Lord is shallow,
A mere show before the world.
If the Lord has not shown himself to us,
All talk is fruitless, says Tuka.
Until the Lord and the devotee look at each other within,
We cannot say that they have met.

na ye netra jal, Gatha 82

---

* **Sandalwood** paste, which is very costly, is used for cooling the body.

None Will Help You at the Time of Death

Even if you have great and powerful friends,
None of them will help you at the end.
So above all repeat the Lord's Name
And store up your treasure;
Otherwise death will
Gnash its teeth in anger and treat you cruelly.
However much wealth you may collect,
It will all be left behind
And Kal will take it from you.
You may have an army of relatives,
But none of them will be of any use to you
At the time of death.
You can boast about your wealth,
But only until Kal approaches.
O my loved one, work to free yourself
From the wheel of eighty-four, says Tuka.

maitra kele mahaabali, Gatha 86

Toiling Like a Bullock

In this world we get a grain of happiness
And a mountain of misery –
Remember this and follow the teachings of the saints.
Half this life is spent in sleeping –
Some in childhood,
Some in old age with all its illnesses.
O foolish one, if you don't meditate now, says Tuka,
You will return again and again in other lives,
Toiling like a bullock who, with blinders on,
Walks round and round an oil press.

sukh paahata java paade, Gatha 88

Ceremonies Only Strengthen Ego

What is the use of burning sesame and rice
In religious ceremonies
When lust and anger are still there within you?
This is not devotion to the Lord.
You are taking trouble over all these ceremonies
And all this recitation of scriptures
Just to raise your social standing.
All these ceremonies and pilgrimages
Have only strengthened your ego.
Giving alms and sharing your wealth
Have also increased your ego.
Tuka says, your whole approach is wrong.
You have not repeated the Lord's Name,
So you have gained nothing.

til juulile tuundul, Gatha 90

Redeemer of the Distressed

O Lord, I have been caught up in serving my family
And am burning in the misery of this world,
So now I am turning to you –
O my mother, come and save me!
I am weighed down by the karmas of many lives
And don't know how to escape from it all.
Inside and outside, I am surrounded by robbers;
Nobody has any pity on me.
I am crippled, I am plundered,
I have been in distress for so long.
O my Lord, redeemer of the distressed,
Be true to your name,
Come quickly and save me, says Tuka.

sansaartaape taapalo me deva, Gatha 91

Worldly Life Is a Mirage

A mirage looks very real even though it is not,
And so the deer runs after it,
Hoping for water until the effort almost kills it.
O fools, when you know that worldly life is a mirage,
Why are you destroying yourselves?
Think of your own good and don't delay.
Our stored karmas will take us
From this life to another one,
Where our own actions will bear fruit.
You can boast and brag, says Tuka,
But in the end you'll be taken to the crematorium
And fire will reduce you to ashes.

mrugjal dise saachpana aise, Gatha 99

It Is Never Too Late

My advice to you all is to stop wasting your lives;
I fall at your feet to advise you to cleanse your hearts.
Only concentrating your mind
And meditating on his Name will help you.
Engage yourself in a business that will profit you.
What else can I teach you? asks Tuka.

aata tari pudhe, Gatha 101

From the Gallows to a Pinprick

Put all honour and dishonour to one side.
Then you will always be content
And you will find happiness in the Lord's darshan.
Peace will reign within you,
And Kal will lose his hold on you.
When your past actions catch up with you,
Face them bravely, says Tuka.
Know that it could have been much worse.

maan apamaan gove, Gatha 109

When the Mind Cooperates

When the mind cooperates,
Very little effort is needed for God-realization.
One who is not affected by happiness and misery
Is fit to meet the Lord –
This is the gist of all spiritual methods.
You don't have to search far and wide –
Just know that your worldly attachments are false,
And don't be so concerned about your body, says Tuka.

thode aahe thode aahe, Gatha 110

Company of Saints or Pilgrimages?

In places of pilgrimage
They worship water and stones,
But with saints, you'll find God himself.
So, when in the company of a saint,
Offer yourself completely to him.
At places of pilgrimage, only those who have
Deep devotion gain something,
But at the feet of the saints
Even fools will get salvation.
Know that one who is free of the three afflictions[*]
Is free of all sin, says Tuka.

tirthi dhonda paani, Gatha 114

---

[*] **three afflictions:** 1) *aadhyaatmika*—proceeding from intrinsic causes such as disorders of body and mind; 2) *aadhibhautika*—proceeding from extrinsic causes such as people, animals, inanimate objects and forces of nature; 3) *aadhidaivika*—proceeding from supernatural causes such as planetary movements, witchcraft or supernatural beings.

Let Go!

When the monkey puts his hand into the neck of the jar
And holds the food tight, he cannot take it out.
What a pity; he does not see
That he has to let the food go,
And so he is caught by the trapper.
The parrot sits on the fowler's revolving pipe,
Which turns him upside down.
Fearing that he may fall into the water below,
Forgetting that he could just let go
And take wing, he too is caught.
So is it with us.
When we hold the world tight, says Tuka,
How can we hope for liberation?

maakade muthi dharile phutaane, Gatha 132

It Won't Take a Second

I have rid you of all troubles and set you free –
Now just keep repeating the Lord's Name.
When you repeat his Name constantly,
No sins will stay with you.
Even if you have millions of sins,
It won't take a second for the Lord's Name
To burn them away.
Don't worry about your sinchit karmas* –
I will stand as a guarantor for them.
Kal has no access to the place
Where the Lord's Name exists, says Tuka,
Because there sins are reduced to ashes.

chaal kelaasi mokala, Gatha 134

---

* **sinchit karmas:** the store of unpaid past karmas. It is from this store that the fate karmas in succeeding lives are drawn.

No Outward Show Will Help

When your heart is not pure,
It is no use bathing in the Ganges
Or making a pilgrimage to Banaras,
For an extra-hard grain never softens
However much you boil it.
If there is no love and devotion in your heart,
No outward show will help,
Whether it be a mark on the forehead
Or a chain of beads.*
However much you talk about the Lord,
If there is no love, admonishes Tuka,
It will be no better than the barking of a dog –
You will just be wasting your energy.

kaa'e kaashi kariti ganga, Gatha 137

---

* Sadhus often put a mark on the forehead, sometimes with ashes, or some
wear beads as an outward sign of their renunciation of the world.

Without These Eyes and Ears

Without these eyes, I have seen everything inside.
I have dropped all thought of 'me' and 'mine',
So now I feel at one with all.
Without the use of these hands and feet,
Within I have everything.
In this world I have no interest in food,
But inside I have had my fill.
I talk very little here, but there I speak
The unspoken language,
And whatever was hidden is revealed.
Without these ears I have heard the divine music,
Which has stilled my mind, declares Tuka.

na dekhon kaahi, Gatha 249

Even the Gods Want a Human Birth

Even the gods in the heavens want a human birth.
We are lucky to have been given this body
So that we can be his devotees.
We should take advantage of this life
To reach the highest spiritual region.
We will take the ladder to the heavens
And climb it step by step, says Tuka.

ihalokicha ha dehe, Gatha 254

Longing for Home

Like a child bride sitting in a bullock cart
As she goes to her husband's house
Casting tearful glances back towards her old home,*
That is my condition, O Lord.
When will I meet you?
I am yearning for you, my Lord,
Like a child parted from its mother,
Weeping in distress and longing for her.
I am like a fish in agony,
Longing for water, says Tuka.

kanya saasuryaasi jaaye, Gatha 266

Practice Makes Perfect

By taking a little each day,
One gets used to digesting a poisonous root
Which others dare not even look at.
By practising every day, some manage to hold
Poisonous serpents in their hands
Which others tremble even to look at.
The impossible is made possible by effort.
So it is with regularity in meditation, says Tuka.

saadhuni bachanaag, Gatha 298

---

* In villages, a girl would often be married at nine or ten years of age and would travel by bullock cart to her in-laws' home. After that, she would see her family only on special occasions or by special invitation.

Hollow Talk

You are making me talk about spirituality, O God,
So please let me experience it too
Or I will be exposed to ridicule.
I shall be like fine food without salt,
Or a corpse dressed in finery,
Or an actor who acts badly,
Or a beautiful person with ugly behaviour, says Tuka.
My condition is like a marriage ceremony of dolls,
Which is useless however lavishly you spend on it
I don't find any real love and devotion within me.

bolavisi taise aani anubhava, Gatha 304

In My Dream

In my dream, it seemed that I was being held for ransom,
But it turned out to be just a hoax.
All for nothing I cried out for help
To take me out of my troubles.
I saw rich men, poor men and kings,
But on waking, realized none of them existed.
I suffered much, and it was all real enough,
But that was when I slept.
Now my experience tells me the truth –
Through miseries in my dream, my eyes have opened.
The saints have warned me, says Tuka;
Otherwise my mouth would never have opened
To repeat the Lord's Name.

svapnichiya goshti, Gatha 336

Only Meditation Will Lead to Liberation

If the smell of food could satisfy hunger,
Why would food be cooked in every home?
If a glance at water could quench thirst,
Why would water be stored in every home?
Looking at the shade of a tree gives no relief
Until one sits under it.
Songs about the glory of the Lord
Bear fruit only if there is firm faith in the heart.
Just knowing about the path leads nowhere –
Only meditation will lead to liberation.
Think of your own welfare, says Tuka –
Repeat the Lord's Name incessantly.

annaachya parimale jari jaay bhook, Gatha 342

A Real Saint

A real saint is one who befriends
Those tormented by sorrow and suffering,
And he is the one in whom the Lord lives.
A saint's heart is like butter, soft both inside and out.
He holds close to his heart those with no other support
And is as merciful and kind to his servants
As to his own children.
How can I adequately describe such a One,
Who is the very image of the Lord himself, says Tuka.

je ka ranjale gaanjale, Gatha 347

So Leave All Else

Walking on the path of my formless God
I have easily become blind to worldly things.
My outward tendencies have turned inwards
And I am no longer interested in the physical world.
All feelings of 'me' and 'mine' have disappeared,
And the things that seem all-important in this world
No longer matter.
So now I repose in a state of bliss,
Free from all illusion.

At the peak of Trikuti, I received without effort
The rare gift of the Lord's grace.
I have cast off my load of worldly desires
And my karmas – good and bad.
I am beyond the turmoil of the three gunas
And I know that I need not beg anymore
For the satisfaction of my worldly desires.
I have attained the highest knowledge
And all my desires have been fulfilled.

I turned my attention inwards and upwards
And listened to the music of Soham.
When I was pulled by it,
The formless One revealed himself.
He bestowed on me the gifts of
His own essence and true knowledge.
He united me with himself
And kept a distinction only in name.
The Shabd is truly the essence of everything,

It is a treasure trove of goodness in action,
It is the greatest gift which can be given.

For aeons this has been the path of God-realization.
Many a one has swum across
Through devotion to Shabd.
Rest assured that this is the only secret.
Without the knowledge of this truth
The devotee can never attain his goal.
So leave all else and devote yourself to the Shabd
With one-pointed attention.
This is the path that saints have followed
Since time immemorial, says Tuka.

sahaj mi aandhala ga, Gatha 426

Come One, Come All!

I have girded up my loins to fight Kal bravely,
I have built a road to cross this ocean of existence.
Come one, come all, young and old,
Men and women, people of any status.
Nobody need think about anything,
Nobody need worry about anything.
Whether you are too busy with your work
Or you have no work, come all –
Even you who are doing penances or sacrifices.
Come, you who have some spiritual attainment,
Come, you who desire spiritual attainment –
I am giving a trumpet call to all!
Only the currency of the Lord's Name
Will help you there.
The Lord has sent me to this world
As bearer of his Name.

kaas ghaaloni balkat, Gatha 519

Drummer of Devotion

I am at home in the highest region,
Yet I have come to this world
For the sake of humankind.
I advise the world to act with real devotion
On the teachings of the sages of old.
The world has fallen by the wayside
And dust has been gathering
On the path they revealed.
I will clear the path.
I will use the teachings they left behind.
The real meaning of the scriptures has been lost,
Destroyed by worldly discussions.
Minds have been filled with lust and greed
So the mystic methods have been drowned.
But I have come to beat the drum of devotion,*
To make Kal tremble, says Tuka.
So now enjoy the advent of the Lord's Name.

aamhi vaikunthvaasi, Gatha 520

---

* **drum of devotion:** It was common practice in villages to draw attention to announcements by playing a *dholak,* a cylindrical drum tapered on both ends.

In the World but Not of It

I speak the unspoken language,
I have died to live.
Though living among people,
I am, in truth, not with them.
I appear to enjoy the things of the world,
Yet my mind is not in it.
I am in the world but not of it –
I have broken free of all attachments and desires.
I am not what I appear to be, says Tuka.
You may ask the Lord about my real condition.

bolo abolane maroneeya jine, Gatha 537

No Other Method Works

In Kaliyug no other method works,
So hold firmly to the Lord's feet and repeat his Name.
All merits come with this and it destroys all sins –
You become worry-free.
The Lord's Name saves men and women alike.
All times are good for repeating his Name,
Which puts an end to the miseries of birth and death –
You do not have to give up a normal life for this.
For those who want it, this is my advice –
Repeat the Lord's Name with devotion.

aanik kaahi na chaale upaay, Gatha 542

Only You

If ever I praise someone else,
Let my tongue wither away, O Lord.
If ever I am attracted to someone other than you,
Let my head be cut off.
If my eyes look fondly at any but you,
Let them be blinded at once.
What use are these ears of mine, O Lord,
If they do not hear the nectar of the inner music?
What use am I, asks Tuka,
If I forget you even for a moment?

tujavin vaani aanikaanchi thori, Gatha 565

Feelings of Love

I have all that I ever desired
And there is nothing more to say.
I have made contact with the Lord's Name
And now nothing else matters.
What can I say? I am like someone
Who has eaten a sweet but cannot speak.
It is better that I stay silent, says Tuka.

icchaave te javali aale, Gatha 574

Cultivate Serenity

In this world there is no happiness like serenity;
All else brings misery in its wake.
So let your mind be serene
And you are sure to cross over
To the other side of the ocean of existence.
If you feel lust and anger stirring within you,
Your life will be filled with physical and mental troubles.
If you cultivate serenity,
All afflictions will vanish, declares Tuka.

shaantiparate naahi sukh, Gatha 580

More Precious Than Empires

Real devotees look down even upon Brahma's kingdom,
For they have the treasure of repeating the Lord's Name.
They regard Indra's opulence
Not as pleasure but as disease;
They have no interest
In being emperor of the whole world,
And they would count it a misfortune
To rule the netherworld.
They see the falseness and futility of supernatural powers
Obtained through mystical practices, says Tuka.
They see even salvation as misery, not happiness.
Everything is disgusting and useless to them
Except the Lord.

parameshthipada tuchha kariti, Gatha 582

I Can Do Nothing

I want to devote myself to you, but I lack love –
All my attempts to sit at your feet have come to naught.
For some reason my mind is out of control.
When I wish to do good deeds, I lack will power;
When I wish to give in charity, I lack the means;
I do not know how to honour priests and guests.
I have no mercy for my fellow humans in my heart,
Nor can I do anything for them.
I do not know how to surrender to my Master,
Nor how to serve the saints.
I cannot perform rites and rituals,
Nor can I renounce the world.
I cannot go to dwell in forests,
Nor can I control my senses.
When I wish to make pilgrimages, my heart is not in it;
When I wish to make vows, I do not know how.
Even though I say that God resides within me,
The feelings of 'me' and 'you' still remain.
All these weaknesses have led me to surrender to you.
I have no more worries now, says Tuka,
Since I have no need of past merits*
And I have become your marked servant.

maaza tava khuntala upaav, Gatha 648

---

* Since he is already marked, he doesn't have to be concerned whether his deeds give him enough credit to find a Master.

Fulfilment

I have crossed the ocean of life —
That is the truth.
Your Name is forever on my lips
And I have severed all links with worldly life.
Nothing can ever come in my way now, says Tuka,
And nothing other than you remains for me.

utarlo paar satya jhaala ha nirdhaar, Gatha 763

Respect the Human Body

Look upon this human body with great respect,
For within it lies the Name
That leads to permanent happiness.
When duality vanishes, the Lord is seen
And the self merges in the Lord.
People make offerings, take vows and endure penances,
But they lose their due reward
Because they crave things other than the Lord.
Tuka says: give up all wanderings
And know that permanent happiness
Lies within you.

deh ha saadar pahaava, Gatha 808

Only through Love and Devotion

O Lord, your form is beyond thought and speech –
Devotion is the only means I have of knowing you.
I weigh you in the scales of love, O infinite One –
There is no other way to grasp your true state.
You cannot be realized through physical means,
All rituals, penances and yogic exercises are useless,
Nor can you be found through intellect and reason.
O Lord, please accept service from
My simple but loving heart, prays Tuka.

manwaachaateet tuze he swaroop, Gatha 810

The Lord Will Be Your Minstrel

Does worldly opinion matter
When your heart has witnessed the Truth?
You should look to your own welfare.
True love means knowing that
The Lord is everywhere, within and without.
Pure love needs no words
Because it can be felt by others.
A devotee is concerned only with inner bliss;
No lures of this world can entice him.
The Lord himself becomes the minstrel
And sings the praises
Of one who has pure devotion, says Tuka.

chitta gwaahi tethe laukikaache kaa'e, Gatha 951

Only for the Benefit of Others

In this creation, I have been smaller than an atom,
But now I have merged into Him
And expanded to the outer limits of space.
I have swallowed my ego
And with it my worries about the body,
Which in any case is illusion personified.
Now that I have discarded the three coverings,[*]
The eternal flame is shining within me.
My life's aim is achieved, declares Tuka;
Now I exist only for the benefit of others.

anuraniya thokada Tuka aakaashaaevadha, Gatha 993

Pangs of Separation

My soul is suffering without you,
Like a fish out of water, writhing in agony.
Without you I am distressed,
Like a person who cannot find his buried treasure,
Or an infant weeping and wailing for his lost mother.
Such, O Lord, is my anguish without you –
How many such examples shall I give you?
Shelter at your feet is the only cure.
A gnawing fear grips my heart –
That the Lord may have forsaken me.
You know my condition, says Tuka,
So pray take pity on me.

jeevanaavaachuni talamale maasa, Gatha 1031

---

[*] **three coverings:** physical, astral and causal bodies.

A Father's Responsibility

If the son of a nobleman is poor and unkempt,
Who else but his father will be the laughing stock?
It may be the son who is ugly or ill-behaved,
But it is his father who will have to take care of him.
I am a sinner, but I am your marked soul, says Tuka,
So it is your responsibility to take care of me.

samarthaache baal kevilvaane dise, Gatha 1055

Entanglement

Attracted by the sound of the snake charmer's pipe,
The snake is caught, placed in a box
And taken from house to house to earn money –
Such is my condition in this world.
O Lord, I beg of you, take me out of this entanglement.
I am helpless; only your mercy can save me.
The fish takes the bait and, once hooked,
Is pulled from the water and killed.
Can its parents help it?
Birds fly back to their nests to care for their young ones.
Their attachments lure them into the hunter's net
And they are caught.
When a fly sits on melted sugar,
Its wings are quickly trapped and
The more it tries to struggle, the more it gets caught.
O Lord, come to my aid –
My desires are killing me.

sarpa bhulon guntale naada, Gatha 1092

Ceaseless Repetition of the Lord's Name

One who repeats the Lord's Name with every morsel
Gets the merit of fasting, even though he eats.
One who repeats the Lord's Name
While doing daily work
Always has the bliss of meditation within him.
One who repeats the Lord's Name while walking
Gets the merit of performing sacrifices at every step.
Blessed is such a body,
It has no need of pilgrimages and vows.
One who repeats the Lord's Name
Both in the enjoyment and sacrifice of worldly pleasures
Is not bound by his actions, declares Tuka.
One who thus repeats the Lord's Name ceaselessly
Is liberated during this very lifetime!

raam mhane graasograasi, Gatha 1096

Banish Worldly Desires

Give up agitation and be still, O mind!
My Lord is all-merciful –
In the end he will give you eternal happiness
And release you from the wheel of eighty-four.
Many a soul will be emancipated in your company,
And thus you will have
Millions of good deeds to your credit.
Repeat constantly the Name of the Lord
To make yourself fit for this world and the next.
Keep away from the lures of desires, says Tuka,
For only then will you attain supreme bliss.

na kari talamal raahe re nischal, Gatha 1143

The Glory of Saints

By the light of the sun, the lamp or the diamond,
We see only what is manifest,
But by the grace of saints
The unmanifested Lord is made visible.
How can a lowly one like me
Dare to describe their greatness,
When their glory is beyond the comprehension
Even of Brahma and the rest?
The fever of bodily afflictions
Can be allayed by sandalwood paste,
But the fires of the three attributes
Can be extinguished only by the company of saints.
Parents lovingly tend to the body of a child
But it is only the company of saints
That frees their child from the wheel of birth and death.
Tasty food stills hunger for a time,
But the words of the saints put an end
To all the agonies of transmigration, declares Tuka,
So don't wait to be invited, but go to the saints.

ravi deep heera daaviti dekhane, Gatha 1260

No Room for Desires

How can there be any room left for worldly desires
When all the time I am engrossed
In remembering your Name?
There is no longer a barrier between us
For the seed of devotion has borne fruit.
With constant repetition of your Name
I have nothing to worry about now.
By the grace of your feet, my Lord,
The illusion of this world has vanished, says Tuka.

kothe bhog urala aata, Gatha 1276

Make Me Humble

Make me small and humble, O Lord,
For only a tiny ant can pick up
Grains of sugar from sand,
While the mighty elephant has to suffer
The prodding of the goad.
Those who hold their heads high
With arrogance and pride
Fall under the ruthless buffets of ill-fortune.
Ponder this, O friend, says Tuka,
And be the lowliest of the low.

lahaanapana dega deva, Gatha 1282

Remember the Last Moment

I am surprised at the people of this world!
How is it that they never think of their own welfare?
They seem so sure of themselves,
But who will help them on their last day?
Why are they so carefree?
What answer will they give to the messenger of death?*
Have they forgotten that they will die?
What are they so pleased about?
What is wrong with them?
Is there anything they cannot do?
Why don't they remember the Lord
And be free from bondage?
It will cost them nothing!
Why do they never think of the Lord?
They have forgotten him, says Tuka,
So now they will have to wander through the four *khanis.*†

vaate ya janaache, Gatha 1496

---

* **messenger of death:** Yamdoot, who takes charge of souls not initiated by a Master at death.
† **four *khanis:*** According to the Hindu traditions, all the creatures of this world originate in four different ways: 1) conceived in the womb *(jeraj)*—mammals; 2) hatched from eggs *(andaj)*—birds and reptiles; 3) born with the change of seasons and decay of organic matter *(setaj)*—insects, worms and parasites; 4) germinated from soil *(utbhuj)*—vegetation.

Saints Live Only for Others

Words fail me –
How shall I sing of the glory of the saints?
It is enough that I have laid my head at their feet.
The philosopher's stone gave up its greatness
When it touched iron
And turned base metal into gold.
Saints come into this world
Only for the benefit of humankind.
For this, they endure bodily hardships –
Kindness is their asset.
Having no concern for themselves,
Saints are happy in the happiness of others, says Tuka,
And nectar flows from their tongues.

kaa'e vaanu aata na pure he vaani, Gatha 1510

Intense Longing

An intense longing for you
Ever resides in my heart.
I have seen your form once
And I am now unable to forget it.
My worldly affairs have ended
Because my attention is ceaselessly fixed on you.
My inner vision is now opened, says Tuka,
And you have revealed yourself to me within.

sarvakaal maaze chitti, Gatha 1515

The Bliss of the Celestial Melody

The outer world has no attraction
For one who is absorbed in the unstruck music.
It is hard then for him
To come down to this gross level.
He is drunk with the celestial melody,
Oblivious of his own body,
Indifferent to worldly suffering and its solace.
The words he now utters are as holy as the scriptures.
When he talks of his bliss
People are in awe of him, but still they doubt his words.
One who has wearied of the charms of this world
Drinks deep the nectar of the divine melody
And attains tranquillity within, says Tuka.

anuhati guntala nene bahyaranga, Gatha 1637

Bathing at Holy Places

What have you gained by pilgrimages to holy places?
You have merely washed the exterior of your body.
In what way has your mind been purified
That such visits may be considered as any merit?
So long as there is no peace, forgiveness and mercy within,
What are you bragging about? asks Tuka.

jaaunia tirtha kaa'e tuva kele, Gatha 1732

Limitless Treasure

The one who is asking for grace has only two hands,
But the Giver has unlimited treasure.
What shall I do?
Where shall I keep my treasure?
O Lord, this is a big problem for me.
The heart that once was mine
Is now overflowing with your love.
My tongue is exhausted from speaking of your gifts.
Let me be whatever I may be, says Tuka,
But let me be always at your feet.

maagtiyaache donich kar, Gatha 1738

Importance of Devotion

The unstruck music reverberates within all beings,
But who can be liberated
Without repeating the Lord's Name?
The Lord is alive within all of us
But we must see him in the Master's form
Before we can swim across.
Knowledge is within us all
But without devotion we cannot know God.
What use are the yogic postures
If there is no light at the third eye?
Don't indulge your body, says Tuka,
For if you do, you will not find God.

anuhat dhwani waahe sakala pindi, Gatha 1789

Theft

The Lord has committed a theft in his own home,
In this human body.
He has emptied out the house
And made himself a pauper.
The pauper runs and runs in search of the robber,
Not knowing which way to go,
Not knowing where to seek the thief.
But the pity of it is that the Lord
Has taken away everything
And hidden himself in the victim's own house.
Nothing now remains in Tuka's home.
But, Tuka asks, since the robber and the robbed are one,
Who has robbed and who has lost?

devaache ghari deve keli chori, Gatha 1840

Be Vigilant

Don't keep on sleeping your life away,
Or at least choose the right time to sleep.
Be careful, alert and remain watchful,
For robbers are ever ready to swoop.
These great cheats are encircling you.
Once you lose the human form
Only distress and misery will be left.
Be ever vigilant, guard your own treasure.
Open your inner ears, says Tuka,
It costs you nothing.

avaghechi nijo naka avagheyi thaa'i, Gatha 1841

101

None Like Him

The Lord is good, the Lord is gracious;
He responds according to the devotee's love.
The Lord is gracious, the Lord is merciful;
His bounty knows no bounds.
The Lord is powerful, the Lord is mighty;
He has no peer in the universe.
I want the Lord, I want him!
He is adored by one and all.
My Lord is great, my Lord is great!
To his feet I cling, says Tuka.

dev bhala, dev bhala, Gatha 1868

Tuka's Lord

The Lord is mine –
He is the very life of all creatures.
The Lord is near –
He is within and without,
He resides in one and all.
My Lord is sweet –
He fulfils the desires of his devotees.
The Lord is my protector,
The Lord is my preserver.
With his grace, death is vanquished, says Tuka.
My Lord is merciful and takes care of me.

dev aamcha aamcha, Gatha 1870

Real Wealth

From a tiny ant to a mighty king,
All are alike to me.
Attachments and desires of the world,
Such traps laid by Kal have no hold on me.
Mud and gold are all the same to me
Since ethereal wealth and heavenly bliss
Have come my way, declares Tuka.

mungi ani rao, Gatha 1895

Tuka's Apprehension

O my Lord, how will I know
That you have accepted me as your own?
Why have I experienced nothing?
I search within and find myself just as I always was.
You have decorated me with a spiritual reputation,
But this adornment is a sorrowful burden on my head
While there is still no change within me, says Tuka.

maaza tumhi deva kela angikaar, Gatha 1906

The Eternal Flow of the Lord's Name

Boundless bliss has filled my entire being,
The stream of my love flows swiftly,
And I sing the Lord's Name unceasingly.
The flow of his love and his Name never stops.
It is so strong that it has crossed the barriers
Between this world and the next, says Tuka,
And now both shores look the same to me.

aanandaachya koti sathaulya aamha poti, Gatha 1978

Your Lotus Feet Are My Only Shelter

Your lotus feet are forever within my heart, O Lord,
And they have unfolded the mystery within.
For a spiritually ignorant one like me
Your feet are my only shelter,
And you alone know how to keep me on the path.
My mind is stilled and my senses are subdued –
It is not my strength, but your power
That has made this possible.
I see no difference now between merits and demerits.
The darkness of ignorance has vanished
And I have gone beyond the three attributes.
O Lord, I sought protection at your feet
And now I recognize, says Tuka,
That this is all due to your power.

tuze paaya maaze raahiyele chitti, Gatha 1999

My Constant Companion

With love you lead me by the hand
And stay with me wherever I go.
Your support alone keeps me treading the path of life.
You have taken over all my responsibilities;
It is you who give meaning to my foolish chatter.
You have removed my inhibitions
And made me fearless and bold.
All humankind is now my guardian;
They are all my kith and kin and loved ones.
As I enjoy your love, says Tuka,
There is bliss within me and all around me.

jethe jaato tethe tu maaza saangaati, Gatha 2000

On God-Realization

The treasure I have found will never be exhausted;
I have sacrificed myself to find it.
Meditation has cleared my store of karmas
And I am no longer attached to my actions
Since a dam of perseverance has been built
To stop their flow.
Heat and cold, sorrow and joy no longer affect me;
I am calm now, both within and without.
The cycle from seed to plant to seed is all over now –
All finished, all destroyed.
Out there in the world,
Seeds will go on living and dying,
But I am attached to the Lord's Name, says Tuka.

jodile te aata na sare saarita, Gatha 2008

Humility

Why should I judge others' merits or faults –
Don't I have enough of my own?
Why should I assess others' virtues and vices –
Do I have fewer than they have?
Why should I dwell on others' malice and rancour?
I have even more of these failings in me!
There is none as deceitful and false as me;
I have yet to see such a one with my own eyes.
I have vices in abundance, says Tuka,
I surrender them at your feet, my Lord.

kaasaya gunadosha paaho aanikaanche, Gatha 2036

106

The Company of Saints

Whatever enters into fire becomes fire
And loses its own nature.
At a single touch of the philosopher's stone
Iron turns into gold and becomes precious to the world.
Rivers, brooks and streams — all flow into the Ganges
And become one with it.
Mere contact with a sandalwood tree
Fills the surrounding plants with the same fragrance.
As for me, says Tuka, I have touched the feet of the saints,
And there is no difference now
Between me and the Lord.

agnimaaji gele agni ho'uni tech thele, Gatha 2051

Saints Are Our Liberators

The joy of repeating the Lord's Name
Will make us dance and clap.
The Lord is kind-hearted and merciful;
He fondly protects those who surrender to him.
He has already liberated countless souls
Who have surrendered to him,
And I am sure that he will liberate me too.
This secret, says Tuka, was given to me by saints.

aamhi naacho tene sukhe, Gatha 2105

107

Plead for Me

O saints, you are ever merciful and righteous.
Pray then, grant me one boon:
Remind the Lord about me,
Plead for me and tell him of my piteous condition.
I am an orphan, a degenerate and a notorious sinner,
But implore him on my behalf
Not to drive me away from his feet.
If you hand me over to the care of the Lord,
He will not ignore or forsake me, says Tuka.

krupaalu sajjan tumhi santajan, Gatha 2256

The Lord's Name Is Unparalleled

Even the gift of this earth, encompassed by the oceans
Will not equal the merit earned
By repeating the Lord's Name.
So don't be lazy, but repeat his Name day and night.
Reciting the Vedas and other scriptures
Touches not even a fringe of the Lord's Name.
Pilgrimages to holy places such as Banaras and Prayag[*]
Cannot be compared to the Lord's Name.
Penances, austerities, or even having oneself cut in half
By the saw of Banaras[†]
Cannot be compared to the Lord's Name.
The Lord's Name is the highest of all practices;
It is the essence of spirituality, says Tuka.

       samudra valyaankit pruthwiche daan, Gatha 2298

---

[*] **Banaras and Prayag:** two of the many places of pilgrimages in India.
[†] **saw of Banaras:** In medieval times, there was a belief that whoever voluntarily sacrificed his life on a special saw kept in the holy city of Banaras would attain salvation after death.

My Death Is Dead

My death is dead and I have become immortal;
All my bodily consciousness has gone
And the very source of death has been annihilated.
There was a flood of passions in my life,
But now it has ebbed and I face this life with calmness.
The main aim of my life, says Tuka,
Has been fulfilled in the right manner.

maran maaze maron gele, Gatha 2348

The Holy Confluence

Satsang is the confluence of three holy rivers –
The Lord, the saint and the Name.
There the very dust of the saint's feet
Is sacred and hallowed.
When people listen to satsang with reverence,
Mountains of sins are burnt off and they become pure.
The holy places themselves come to satsang to become holier–
Auspicious indeed is every moment spent at a saint's feet.
Beyond compare is this glorious confluence
Of the Lord, the saint and the Name.
It cannot be described even by Brahma, says Tuka.

katha triveni sangam, Gatha 2357

The Treasure Is Within

Grasp the treasure of Nam and be immortal –
It costs you nothing.
There will be no more births,
As mountains of sins will be burnt away.
With boundless love and devotion
Sing the Name of the Lord
And gather the treasure of Nam in abundance.
The treasure lies within your own home, says Tuka,
So do not tire yourself searching for it all over the world.

phukaache te luta saar, Gatha 2393

The Easiest Way

Repeating the Lord's Name
Is a very easy way to find God –
It burns away the sins of entire lifetimes
And you don't have to hide away in a forest.
There is no such difficulty
For the Lord himself comes joyfully to your own home.
Stay seated in your place, concentrate
And call out to the Lord with all your heart –
Ceaselessly repeat the Name given by your Master.
I can swear by the Lord that there is no easier way.
Wise is the one who satiates himself
In this manner, says Tuka.

naam sankirtan saadhan pa'i sope, Gatha 2458

Why Are You Looking Elsewhere?

Why perform mountains of penances?
Why all these rituals?
They only heap misery upon you!
Why roam about in holy places looking for Him?
You will only store up more rewards for another life!
Why worship all these gods and goddesses?
You will get no satisfaction from it!
Why are you taking such pains to achieve salvation
When it will be given free of charge at the Master's feet?
Be occupied only with the Lord's meditation and
You will receive whatever you desire in your house itself.

kaasaya karaave tapaache dongar, Gatha 2469

Merged in You

When salt is dissolved in water,
Can one be distinguished from the other?
So have I become one with you;
My soul has lost itself in you.
When camphor is put into fire,
Not a bit of ash remains.
So has the flame of my soul
Merged into your light, says Tuka.

lavan melavita jale, Gatha 2486

112

A Saint Is Not an Ordinary Human Being

Curds are churned into butter and buttermilk
But do not expect both at the same price.
Both the moon and the stars are in the sky
But do not regard them as equals.
Both diamonds and flintstones lie in the earth
But they cannot be compared.
The saint and ordinary people both live here,
But, says Tuka,
Do not show them the same devotion.

dahyaacheeye angi nighe taaka loni, Gatha 2492

Cleansed by Your Love

O my Lord, my being had lost its purity,
But your Name has made it shine again.
My heart has been cleansed by your love
And repentance has purified me.
My pralabdh karma troubles me no more.
I have surrendered myself at your feet
And fulfilled my promise to you, says Tuka.

jaali hoti kaaya, Gatha 2502

Remember Him Alone

O mind, allow me to remember nothing
That will take me away from the Lord's feet.
Let my tongue repeat only his Name
And my ears hear only his Name.
Let me not bear ill will towards anyone
For it brings nothing but misery.
Let my mind be always calm –
Peace and forgiveness are a great strength.

chitta aisi nako deu aathavan, Gatha 2527

The Nectar of Your Lotus Feet

The nectar of your lotus feet
Is more cooling than coolness itself.
I drink it deep and pour it over my head;
It cleanses me of all my shortcomings.
All my sins have been destroyed
By the holy waters of your feet.
Sitting at the Lord's feet,
Tukaram is immersed in the surging wave
Of the divine Sound.

sheetal te sheetalaahuni, Gatha 2542

Where Is the Question of Duality?

The sea and the sky have united,
Each lost in the other.
Where is the question of duality
When the waves have merged into the ocean?
When each has lost itself in the other
How can there be ebb and flow?
My object is achieved, says Tuka,
And my births and deaths have come to an end.

nabhomay jaale jal, Gatha 2587

Come Quickly, My Lord!

My heart is in deep and constant anguish
Forever pining for your lotus feet.
Come to me, come quickly, my Lord!
Hold me close and grant me happiness.
I am waiting for you with a restless heart,
Trying to remember what my faults could be.
O breath of my life, my Lord, says Tuka,
Hasten and reveal yourself.

kshana kshana jeeva vaatatase khanti, Gatha 2593

You Alone Are Everything to Me

You are my beloved mother;
You are my only shelter –
O Lord, I am eagerly awaiting your arrival.
You alone are my father and my son;
You alone are the one closest to my heart.
I have offered you my heart and my soul –
Without you everything seems barren, says Tuka.

tu maazi maauli, tu maazi saauli, Gatha 2607

Dying While Living

I experienced my own death –
It was a festive occasion beyond compare.
Now my joy fills all the three worlds
And I rejoice in being a part of the universal soul.
Till now I was confined to this world alone;
Ego was the barrier separating me from the Lord.
Now that I am devoid of ego, my joy knows no bounds –
Gone forever is the mire of birth and death,
And I am free of the restrictions of 'me' and 'mine'.
Now the Lord lets me live in his house
And my love abides in him.
Whatever I have experienced within, says Tuka,
I now reveal to the world.

aapule maran paahile mya dola, Gatha 2669

Spiritual Treasure

There is none in this world who does not want
Children, wife and wealth,
Even though they are the cause
Of his misery and suffering.
A sick man takes bitter herbs
To be rid of his suffering and pain,
Even though it gives him no pleasure.
Those who run after a thief
Are not chasing him for their enjoyment,
So don't stand in their way.
Each of us knows what he needs to do
So nobody should try to stop him.
Sacrifice yourself, says Tuka
And you'll obtain the spiritual treasure.

aisa koni naahi hen jaya naavade, Gatha 2683

The End Is Drawing Nigh

Old age brings greying hair at my temples,
Which whispers that my date with death
Is drawing near.
O mind, wake up now
And know that your life's objective can be achieved
Only through the practice of Shabd.
In no time the last moment will come
And you will be drowned, warns Tuka.
So do your meditation, for the end is drawing nigh.
Ignore all the useless words around you
And devote yourself only to the Lord's Word.

jara karnamooli saango aali goshti, Gatha 2686

Beg for the Lord Alone

Do not give me any offspring, O Lord,
Lest I get attached to them and forget you.
Do not give me wealth and prosperity, O Lord,
Lest I be burdened with anxiety and care.
Rather, make me a beggar at your door, says Tuka,
So that your Name is always on my lips.

naka deu deva poti he santaan, Gatha 2863

Freedom from Karmas

The Lord himself is now my sinchit,
Pralabdh and kriyaman karmas.*
These karmas cannot touch me now –
I am free from the effects of old age and death.
In unity, as in diversity,
The Lord himself is all-pervading.
The Lord, says Tuka, is ever at play within me.

sanchit, praarabdh, kriyaamaan, Gatha 2932

A Puppet

My ego is dead and
I have surrendered my body to the Lord.
Now there is no question of my serving anybody.
The Lord is pulling the strings of this marionette show
And this puppet is dancing to his tune.
I say only what the Lord makes me say;
I have no room within for any doubt.
I have surrendered myself to him
And he alone knows
Whether my deeds are good or bad –
That is no longer my concern.
O people of the world, listen:
I am free from the bonds of my body, says Tuka.

aamhi melo tenvha deha dila deva, Gatha 2947

---

* **sinchit (sanchit):** karmas from past lives that are stored; **pralabdh (prarabdh):** karmas from the past that must be gone through in the present life; **kriyaman:** karmas created in the present life.

The Inner Quality

The outer form of musk is unsightly
But within it lies true fragrance.
The same can be said of sandalwood trees which,
Though not beautiful, are valued for their scent.
The philosopher's stone has no claim to beauty
Yet its touch turns iron into gold.
The sword, once smelted, declines in value,
But its original form is worth much, much more.
Caste and creed count for nothing, says Tuka,
Glory to those who repeat the Lord's Name.

kasturiche rup ati heenavar, Gatha 2984

Saints' Words Are Like Nectar

Saints are like the nectar plant
And their words, like its fruit,
Are sweet and beneficial.
O Lord, let me keep their company
For their very speech is full of kindness.
Just as good food cools the system,
Providing good health and lustrous skin,
And the fragrance of the sandalwood tree
Permeates the trees surrounding it,
So too do we absorb
The qualities and virtues of saints, says Tuka.

amrutaachi phale amrutaachi veli, Gatha 3045

The Power of the Lord's Name

What could not be understood in any other way
Can be grasped by uttering the Lord's Name,
What was invisible before
Will become visible by uttering the Name,
What was unutterable before
Will find expression on repeating the Name,
And the One who could not be found before
Will himself come to meet you on repeating the Name.
What was impossible to obtain
Can be obtained in plenty now
Through ceaseless repetition of the Name.
Human beings are completely caught
In the web of attachments, declares Tuka.
But they will be saved through repetition of the Name.

na kale te kalo ye'eel ugale, Gatha 3047

The Wave and the Ocean

The tree is in the seed
And the seed is in the tree.
So is it with you and me, O Lord –
We are merged into one another.
The wave that forms from the ocean
Is one with the ocean.
The object and its reflection, says Tuka,
Are now united.

taruvar beeja poti beej, Gatha 3069

Beasts of Burden

The bullock carries sacks of sugar on its back
But has to be content with eating fodder.
Camels carry boxes of precious goods
But alas, they can only eat thorns.
Worldly pursuits are futile,
For they just add to your desires –
They entangle you even more in the net of your karmas
And hand you over to Kal.
He who takes advantage of this human life
Must recognize its real worth –
Everyone else is wasting their time here.
It is time to be wise, you ignorant fool, warns Tuka,
And step off the cycle of birth and death.

saakarechya gony bailaachiye paathi, Gatha 3070

The Ladder of Nam

If one is attached to the Name of the Lord,
The mesh of illusion is cut asunder
And the ocean of existence evaporates.
Which brave one, in this Kaliyug,
Has been saved through rites and rituals?
It is difficult to read the Vedas and study the scriptures –
Better to repeat constantly the Name of the Lord.
Yogic practices are difficult to perform
And renunciation is not easy –
Better to tread the path of devotion
In the company of saints.
Do not involve yourself in religious ceremonies
Or concern yourself with philosophizing.
Instead, ascend by the easy method of inner Sound.
The only way to eternal peace
Is the practice of the Lord's Name.
This secret has been revealed by the saints, says Tuka.

tute maayaajaal vighade bhavasindhu, Gatha 3113

The Lord's Reflection

For me, the whole of humanity has become the Lord
So my virtues and defects have disappeared.
This is excellent; it makes my heart content.
The reflection in the mirror appears as a separate being,
But the viewer and the image are one and the same.
When the stream merges into the ocean,
It becomes the ocean itself, says Tuka.

dev jaale awaghe jan, Gatha 3132

The Golden Opportunity

The vine of the Lord's Name has spread far and wide
And it sways with fruit and flowers in abundance.
O my dear mind, be like a bird
And satisfy your hunger and thirst now.
The fruit has the sweetness of the first seed,
So feast on it and enjoy it.
Make haste, says Tuka, every moment is precious,
So eat now, while you can.

harinaam veli paavali vistaar, Gatha 3254

My Only Desire

Why should I ask for anything from anyone
As the One I would want to beg from is within me?
If I asked for Indra's position, it would be transitory.
If I coveted Dhruva's place in the sky,*
What would be the use of it,
For he is attached to this destructible creation.
If I desired the pleasures of paradise,
Then after my allotted time
I would again have to return to this world.
If I prayed for immortality,
I would remember that in reality
The soul is already immortal.
The union of the soul with the Lord is unbreakable,
Says Tuka; hence, the only thing I ask for is that.

kaa'e maagaave kavanaasi, Gatha 3380

---

* **Indra:** According to Hindu scriptures, Indra is the ruler of paradise.
Dhruva: A great devotee of Vishnu, Dhruva was granted a place in the firmament as the North Star because of his devotion.

Signs of the Advent of the Lord

When the Lord comes to dwell within us
Our nature changes.
The Lord takes away all our possessions
To show us that nothing exists but him.
He no longer keeps us entangled in
Desires and attachments.
He stops us from talking too much
To keep us away from falsehood.
The Lord destroys our web of illusion
And makes us realize his omnipresence.
The Lord has occupied Tuka's heart by force
And blessed him with all these signs of his presence.

devaachi te khun aala, Gatha 3446

My Body Vacated

Once my body was vacated,
The Lord was enthroned within me.
The care of my entire being
Rests fully with him.
Because of the death of my ego
The Lord has taken up residence in me
And the unquenchable flame shines there.
But, says Tuka, do not think that all this
Has taken place at one stroke.

eka vele kele rite kalivar, Gatha 3502

The Generosity of Saints

How can I say enough about the generosity of saints?
They are the ones who keep me ever vigilant.
How can I repay them for the blessings they bestow?
Even the offering of my life is not payment enough.
Their every utterance is made to help us;
They spare no pains to make us understand.
As the mother cow fondly cherishes her calf,
So do the saints forever protect me, says Tuka.

kaa'e saango aata santaanche upakaar, Gatha 3656

The Lord's Will

By laying my heart at your feet
And putting my full trust in you,
I have now become carefree.
I have made a firm resolve
That whether I am saved or drowned
I will act only as you advise.
I don't know how you have entranced me,
But I will willingly take whatever you give.
O Lord, please don't let me ask anything of you,
But show me how to remain in your will.
Should I struggle to do something,
Or just see what comes?
Pray, guide me, O Lord, says Tuka.

vishvaas dharuni raahilo nivaant, Gatha 3808

127

Stop Running

O mind, stop running after the attractions of the senses
And lie hidden at the Lord's feet.
There you will find happiness and joy
That will not fade, even after aeons.
You will be free from the cycle of birth and death
Without going through mountains of penances.
I have only one thing to tell you, warns Tuka:
Consider wealth and women to be poison.
I shall certainly be grateful to you if you do this,
And we will both go beyond the ocean of existence.

devaachee'e paayi de'i mana budee, Gatha 3810

You Took Away My Heart

My Lord, no doubt you gave me my love for you,
But you took away my heart –
So now we are quits.
Why should I call you generous?
You took one thing from me
And gave me one thing in return.
But you gave me just a little love
And took away all of my heart.
All thoughts have ceased except those of you.
Oh my Lord, says Tuka, you have taken away
All that I had – my heart – leaving me
Sad, depressed and longing for more of your love.

deooniya prem maagitale chitta, Gatha 3818

Face to Face

After seeing you face to face,
My eyes cannot look anywhere else.
O Lord, my heart clings to your feet
In a firm embrace, never to let go.
Never again will I be separated from you,
Just as salt, once dissolved,
Cannot be taken out of water.
I have surrendered my soul
At your lotus feet, says Tuka.

tuja paahata saamori, Gatha 3843

He Is Everywhere

My body and mind have been completely transformed
By contemplating upon the Lord.
When 'me' and 'mine' have been lost in the Lord,
What remains to be said?
When the conscious soul
Embraces the superconscious Lord,
Then you find that he is everywhere, says Tuka.
All my tendencies have turned Godwards.
What else can I say!

dhyaani dhyaata pandhariraaya, Gatha 4077

A Prayer

O Lord, bring my mind to such a state
That in men, women and children, I see only you.
Pray do not let lust, envy, anger,
Slander and duality come near me;
Let me see your presence in everyone.
Make me forever indifferent to sense pleasures
And keep my body, mind and soul at your feet.
Help me, by your grace,
To fulfil these wishes, prays Tuka.

nar naari baale avagha naaraayan, Gatha 4113

The Fruit of Constant Repetition

When the Lord's Name is constantly on one's lips
How can one stay caught in illusion?
He who repeats the Name ceaselessly,
Whether walking, talking, eating or sleeping,
Will have the Lord always with him
In the thick of his worldly duties.
The devotion of ceaseless repetition
Is greater than all the heavens.
Through it the devotee becomes the Lord.
Now Tuka has merged in the Lord.

mukhi vitthalaache naam, Gatha 4161

Killing Animals

Sinners don't understand that other creatures
Also have life like them, so they slit their throats.
The Lord is within every being –
Don't they understand that he lives in animals too?
When they can see these creatures screaming in agony,
How can the hands of these heartless ones
Go towards their throats?
Such vile ones will have to suffer, says Tuka,
They will be hurled into the fires of hell.

jeeve jeev nene paapi saarikhaachi, Gatha 4178

A Devotee's Call for Help

My mind is caught in the snares of the world,
Thrown off balance by its attachments.
Pray, deliver me from this predicament, O Lord,
And release me from the bonds that hold me fast.
I am caught in the snares of the world
And estranged from your Name and Form.
Help me to walk with confidence,
For my path is full of obstacles, says Tuka.

chitta guntale prapanche, Gatha 4182

No More Births and Deaths

Forget about the sugar but enjoy its sweetness;
Forget the salt but savour its taste.
Live in the world but don't drown in worldly affairs –
This is the way to God-realization.
Sugar cannot be put back into sugarcane,
Nor will I return to the womb.
The seeds of karma have been burnt to ashes,
So there can be no more births and deaths for me.
Now that my body counts for nothing,
How can I be given any more of these forms?
In every being in this whole world,
Tuka now sees only the Lord.

gul saanduni godi ghyaavi, Gatha 4269

Experience of 'I Am He'

Set aside were the red colours of rajogun,
The white light of satogun,
The pitch-black of tamogun*
And the golden colour of the essence of purity.
My Satguru applied everlasting collyrium to my eyes,
And I was thus endowed with inner spiritual vision.
Gone was the sense of duality,
No more remained the awareness
Of different regions, time or objects.
My soul became pure;
It expanded into the whole universe.
Now the world was filled with Omnipresence
And I experienced 'I am He'.
Having reached the stage of knowing 'I am That',
Tuka has merged in the Lord
And is absorbed in supreme bliss.

rakta shwet krishna peet, Gatha 4313

---

* These are the three gunas or states of being. The red of rajogun is a state
such as anger or lust, the white of satogun a state of virtue or harmony, and
the black of tamogun a state of ignorance or sloth.

Repayment of Loan

Oh Lord, you have taken the loan of my devotion
And mortgaged your lotus feet in return.
My Lord, now pay me interest in the form of your love,
And thus settle my account quickly.
To retain my treasure, I ceaselessly repeat your Name.
The promissory note in the form of Nam is with me,
Pray, decide how you will pay me
According to your sweet will.
Says Tuka: my dear Lord,
My Satguru is himself witness to this loan.

bhaktiroon ghetle maaze, Gatha 4320

Eternal Unity

I have built my home in the realm beyond illusion
And I live there eternally with the formless Lord.
I have merged fully into the incomparable One
And thus attained eternal unity.
My ego is vanquished forever, says Tuka,
And now I am merged in the form which is forever pure.

niranjani aamhi baandhiyele ghar, Gatha 4326

The Futility of Rituals

Why pursue futile rituals and make a show of purity?
When the mind is impure, all these are useless.
What is the use of reciting volumes of scriptures
If there is no change of heart?
What is the use of singing with cymbals and drum
When the divine music is not experienced within?
When you have no experience of what you preach,
Why talk of your knowledge?
Why indulge in pursuit of name and fame?
This ego is no good for you, says Tuka.

kaa'e ba karisi sovale ovale, Gatha 4332

At the Master's Feet

I bowed down at my Master's feet
And he raised me lovingly with his own hands.
Filled with love and gratitude, I paid homage to him.
Forever bow to such a beloved Master, says Tuka,
And repeat constantly the Name bestowed by him.

sadguruche charani thevita mastak, Gatha 4335

The Master's Blessings

Thanks to my Master's blessings
My heart is overflowing with joy.
My Master knew what my heart longed for
And he spoke to me fondly and cheerfully.
When my Master spoke to me in his infinite grace,
My mind and heart were filled with bliss, says Tuka.

sadgurune maj aashirvaad dila, Gatha 4336

Never Miss Meditation

Even if you have not eaten for a week,
Do not give up listening to this divine Music.
Even if your head cracks and your body breaks,
Do not give up the repetition of his Name.
Even if your body splits into two,
Do not give up the intoxication of the divine Sound.
When someone is this strong,
Then the Lord will dwell within him forever.

saata divsaancha jari jaala upavaasi, Gatha 4338

Without a Master

Without a Master
All scriptures are like the whispering of ghosts,
Says the sage Vyasa* in his Puranas.
One without a Master is like one
Perpetually in mourning –
Do not even glance at his face.†
No efforts will ever liberate him
From the wheel of births and deaths –
Know that his human life was in vain.
So say the holy books, declares Tuka,
And so said all the saints in history.

sadguru vachuni pretarupa vaani, Gatha 4341

---

* **Vyasa:** the mythical compiler of many important works of Hinduism, such as the *Mahabharata,* Puranas and some commentaries.
† **Do not even glance at his face:** This refers to the traditional Hindu belief that it is inauspicious to look at someone who is in mourning.

The Incomprehensible Lord

Even the Vedas cannot comprehend your greatness,
Oh Lord, so they have fallen silent.
My mind, which normally
Runs like the wind in all directions,
Is paralysed and cannot describe you.
If even the sun and the moon
Derive their effulgence from you,
What is the brightness of my intelligence in comparison?
If the thousand-faced one*
Is incapable of describing your greatness,
What chance has a worthless one like me to do so?
I am your helpless infant and you my dear mother.
Therefore, O my beloved Lord, have grace on me
And keep me under your mantle of protection, prays Tuka.

na kale mahima veda maunaavale, Gatha 4363

---

* **thousand-faced one:** most likely refers to Vishnu, the sustainer of the universe, one of the Hindu triad of gods (Brahma, Vishnu and Shiva); or to Sheshnag, the serpent on which Vishnu sleeps during the cosmic night between the last dissolution of the universe and its new manifestation.

The Dust of a Saint's Feet

On contact with the dust of a saint's feet within,
The seeds of desire are easily burnt away.
Then love is created for the Lord's Name
And happiness grows and grows.
My throat is choking with love,
Tears are streaming from my eyes
And the Lord has shown himself to me within.
This path is sweet and simple, says Tuka,
But it is the fruit of past actions.

santacharan raj laagata sahaj, Gatha 4364

You Are My Only Love, O Lord

As the widow who has only one son
Dotes on him day and night,
So too are you my only love, O Lord –
Pray do not send me away.
As a devoted son adores his father,
So do I love you, O Lord.
As the devoted wife loves her husband,
So are you close to my heart, says Tuka.

vidhavesi ek sut, Gatha 4365

139

Why Don't You Respond?

If the river rushes to merge into the ocean
And the ocean refuses to accept her,
Then pray tell me, O Lord,
Where else should she turn?
Can the sea ever be angry with its creatures
And refuse them shelter?
Can the mother refuse shelter to her own child?
Why then, O Lord, are you quiet?
When I have surrendered to you,
Why is there no response? asks Tuka.

ganga geli sindhu paashi, Gatha 4371

Life without Devotion

A life devoid of devotion to the Lord is useless,
Like adorning a corpse with jewels.
Words that speak not of the Lord are as futile
As the jokes of a clown in a serious meeting.
Ceremonies and observations bereft
Of devotion to the Lord are as deceptive
As the softness of a serpent's skin.
Those with no devotion to the Lord
Are unfortunate people.
Tuka asks: what more need I say?

hariwin jine vyarthachi sansaari, Gatha 4391

A Devotee's Despair

You are generous and merciful, a redeemer of sinners!
But all these qualities will be wasted
If you remain beyond my reach.
Scriptures cannot describe your great limits;
All they say is "not this, not that" and remain quiet,[*]
So how can my appeals ever reach you?
Perhaps my past sins are coming in the way.
Has there been some fortunate devotee
About whom I can remind you?
O Lord, do not try my patience, says Tuka,
Pray take heed and make haste to help me.

udaar krupaal patitpaavana, Gatha 4402

Saints Alone Comprehend the Lord

Knowledge of the Ultimate can be obtained
Only through the Satguru –
Comprehension of the Lord's love is beyond us.
Scriptures do not know the true nature of the Lord's love;
Therefore, give up external efforts when you search for God.
Saints alone comprehend the Lord, says Tuka.

guruchiya mukhe hoeel brahmudnyaan, Gatha 4407

---

[*] **not this, not that:** literally, 'not this, not this' (*neti, neti* in Sanskrit); said of God—that he is undefinable.

The True Ship

With hands folded in supplication,
To whom shall I surrender?
Apart from you, is there anyone who will help me?
You are the ocean of mercy,
You are the friend of the humble and the poor
And the redeemer of the world, O Lord!
You are indeed the true ship, says Tuka,
That will carry me across the ocean of existence.

tuj vaachun kona, Gatha 4444

The Lord Is Within

The Lord dwells within the body,
Yet in vain the unfortunate ones seek him outside.
The Lord is alive right inside you,
So why visit these pilgrim centres?
Musk lies in the navel of the musk deer,
But he roams through the forest in search of it.
As sugar is in sugar cane, just so is the Lord in you.
Butter is in milk, but you must know how to churn it.
O ignorant one, says Tuka,
Why don't you seek the Lord within?

dehi asoniya dev, Gatha 4482

Satguru, the Divine Giver

He takes away our attachment
To the transient things and people of this world
And grants us eternal life.
Such is my Satguru, supreme bliss personified!
He shows me sights invisible to these eyes,
He allows me to hear what these ears cannot hear.
What he gives me is beyond imagination
And cannot be put into words,
Held in the hand, or conceived by the mind.
The Satguru is God.
If someone recognizes this one great fact
Then the Satguru will bestow on him
The invaluable treasure of Nam, says Tuka.

ashaashwat gheti shaashwataasi deti
Chhandabaddha Gatha 41

The Lord As a Master

The Lord, who is without attributes,
Comes to this earth as a Master with attributes.
O Lord, take me to the feet of such a one.
The rest of this world seems set apart from God,
But at the feet of the Master there is eternal bliss,
And one feels close to the Lord.
For those who grasp this truth, says Tuka,
Salvation will come with ease.
They need not even wish for it.

dev to sagun sadguru nirgun, Chhandabaddha Gatha 43

143

The Divine Physician

My tongue is intoxicated and satiated
With the holy Name of the Lord.
O divine Giver, please let me remember you always,
So that my mind has no room for sinful thoughts.
Can any disease remain in me
When I have met the divine Physician?
Does not the sun destroy darkness, asks Tuka?

rasana he dhaali
Chhandabaddha Gatha 45

The Human Body Is the Temple of the Lord

The Lord in whom are contained many creations
Dwells within me.
Why search for him in temples
When the human body itself is the temple of the Lord?

Go into that temple,
Meditate there and find the real form of God.
Experience gained through such practice
Makes the devotee realize that the origin of the creation
And the Creator himself are verily within his own being;
They exist within his own soul.
The devotee discovers
That the Lord has neither roots nor branches,
That he has no family name,
That he is beyond comprehension.

Truly, he is permanent and immutable;
The four walls of a temple do not confine him.
Where he is, there is neither time nor timelessness,
Neither emotion nor devotion,
Neither salvation nor liberation,
Neither day, nor night.
My Satguru, Baba Ji, has graciously let me see all this
And made me one with the Lord eternally, says Tuka.

ananta brahmaande jayaache udari
Chhandabaddha Gatha 58

The Primordial Lord

The Lord existed, free of attributes,
When the earth and the firmament did not exist.
The Lord existed, in the region beyond illusion,
When water, fire and light did not exist.
The Supreme Being existed, in his perfection,
When the wind, the sun and the moon did not exist.
My Master, Baba Ji, has showered his grace on me
And merged me into the eternal flame, says Tuka.

jai navhati pruthwi
Chhandabaddha Gatha 71

The Master's Form Within

Concentrate at the tenth door between the two eyes;[*]
Leave your body behind and see the Master's form.
The Master himself will show you
How to recognize this form.
When the all-merciful Lord revealed himself there,
The bubble of illusion was destroyed.
Says Tuka: I serve my Master there without these hands
And I have gone beyond birth and death.

dithi maazi dithi
Chhandabaddha Gatha 74

---

[*] **tenth door:** the eye centre or third eye; the gate through which the soul enters the higher regions. It is called the tenth door in contrast to the nine doors or apertures of the physical body (two eyes, two ears, two nostrils, mouth and the two lower apertures) through which the soul energy dissipates into the world.

Close Your Eyes to See Within

The soul has been cast out into the human body
Where its light can be seen only at the third eye.
The secret of seeing the Lord inside
Is inner concentration and practice.
You can see the Supreme Being
Filling the whole of space,
But you must close both your eyes
And cover them with two fingers.
By contemplating on the darkness, says Tuka,
You will find the Supreme Being seated
Right within your eyes.

chaitanyaachi mus otili sagali
Chhandabaddha Gatha 83

Beyond Soham

At Trikuti, beyond the six chakras,[*]
The beautiful Triveni is flowing.[†]
Many a soul casts off all attributes
And abides here in a state of worship.
Beside Triveni, the divine Sound reverberates,
Sonorous with a higher melody
Coming down from Soham.
Tuka crosses this region and soars upwards
To meet the beloved himself.

shadchakraavari trikuta antari
Chhandabaddha Gatha 88

Inner Light

The sun rises in the midst of darkness –
Pierce through your third eye and see the brightness.
Unless you concentrate at the third eye
You will not see the bright sun within,
Nor will you know yourself.
His form and his light, says Tuka,
Are shining through the whole creation.

aandhaaraache angi prakaashala ravi
Chhandabaddha Gatha 96

---

[*] **chakras:** wheels, centres, ganglions; six energy centres in the human body. The phrase "beyond the six chakras" refers to the inner regions beyond the body.
[†] **Triveni:** the confluence of three currents—Ida, Pingala and Sukhmana. Sukhmana is the central current, the royal highway by which the soul ascends from the eye centre to the higher regions.

Life Is Fleeting

Of what use are the fleeting shadows of the clouds?
They will vanish in a moment.
When has a puppet ever come to life?
Of what use are human bodies and their pleasures?
They are perishable and will be destroyed.
Blessed are the devotees, says Tuka,
Who comprehend this truth.

abhraachi saa'uli upegaasi naye
Chhandabaddha Gatha 101

Lord, the Life of Creation

Tell me: if the soul is removed from the body,
What will be the state of the body?
Tell me: if the thread is taken out of cloth,
What will remain of the cloth?
Tell me: if the water is taken out of hailstones,
What will remain of the hailstones?
Tell me, asks Tuka: without the all-pervading Lord,
What will remain of the creation?

jad shodhoniya chaitanya kaadhile
Chhandabaddha Gatha 102

The Master's Grace

By making me die while living
My Master has given me victory over death
And self-knowledge has dawned within me.
This ancient inflated ego of mine
Has been killed and washed away;
The wounds inflicted on my mind have now been healed.
By giving me the alchemy of the vision of your form,
O my Master, you have made me whole
And freed my body of disease.*
What can I ever offer you in return? asks Tuka.

nijabodh jaala maaziye
Chhandabaddha Gatha 106

Shabd Is God

My house has in it the wealth of Shabd;
The practice of Shabd is my holy scripture;
Shabd is the life of my life.
I will distribute the wealth of Shabd to all.
Know that Shabd is God himself, says Tuka.
I will sing the glory of Shabd and devote myself to it.

aamha ghari dhan,
Chhandabaddha Gatha 128

---

* **disease:** lust, anger, greed, attachment, envy and ego.

A Fundamental Principle

The most sacred place of pilgrimage
Is the feet of the Lord.
Nam, the divine Melody, is the Lord's true form.
Indifference to illusory worldly pleasures is the ablution.*
Awareness of non-duality
And absence of 'mine' and 'thine' is real devotion.
Dislike of worldly life and turning away from it brings
Detachment from everyone and everything of this world.
Absence of the feeling of 'I am the doer'
Brings real happiness.
This principle has been in existence
Since the beginning of time and will continue to exist.
Even the scriptures, says Tuka,
Have propounded this same principle.

tirthaatirtha haripaaya
Chhandabaddha Gatha 375

---

* **ablution:** the ceremonial washing or bathing in holy waters.

The Lord's Grace

Know that it is the Lord's grace
When the mind and intellect
Become engrossed in his contemplation.
Spiritual experience has dissolved my worldly desires,
So now I have turned around and started going up
Towards the path of emancipation.
Concentration on Nam, the form of the Master,
And serving saints have become dear to me.
I have started singing in praise of the Lord's glory.
Says Tuka, it is only the Lord's blessings
On the loving devotee that have brought out in him
These special marks of spirituality.

jaanaavi ti krupa harichi jaahali
Chhandabaddha Gatha 684

True Spiritual Knowledge

Stay in the company of saints
And remain pure and unsullied by worldly attachments.
Freedom from duality is true *brahmadnyan** –
Keep silent until you yourself experience this.
Conquer the senses,
Banish all worldly desires,
Let no doubt ever enter your mind.
For your own spiritual welfare,
Never think that you are separate from the Lord.
Just strive with determination, says Tuka.

karoni satsanga raahe tu nirmal
Chhandabaddha Gatha 719

---

* *brahmadnyan:* Marathi term for the highest spiritual knowledge (*brahmagyan* in Hindi).

Submerged in His Pure Form

Eliminate every desire and doubt from your mind
And get happily engrossed
In the remembrance of the Lord –
Have no thought for anyone else.
With determination remain firm,
Basking in his luminous form.
Numerous doubts will assail your mind,
So pray ardently for the Lord's mercy.
Says Tuka: once you are submerged
In the Lord's pure form,
The Lord's presence alone will be all around you.

sankalpa vikalpa dyaavi tilaanjuli
Chhandabaddha Gatha 733

The Well-Trodden Path

We will search for the path trodden
By those who went before us and we will travel on it.
We will bow at their feet and eat their blessed food.
In this way, all our past karmas will be burnt away
And we will carry with us an immeasurable treasure.
The Lord takes care of orphans like us.
By repeating the Lord's Name
And listening to his Word we only gain,
For our births and deaths come to an end.
This will be an easy path of God-realization.
We will cut into pieces this human existence
And go to our source to rest in comfort, says Tuka.

pudhe gele tyaancha shodhit maarag
Jog Gatha 13

Endnotes

Poems in this book have been translated from the following three books in Marathi:

- *Sartha Tukaram Gatha,* referred to in this book as *Gatha*
- *Sartha Shri Tukaramachi Gatha,* referred to as *Jog Gatha*
- *Shri Tukaram Maharaj Yanchya Abhanganchi Chhandabaddha Gatha,* referred to as *Chhandabaddha Gatha*

For these books, standard poem numbers rather than page numbers are given.

Dedication
vi Make me small and humble, O Lord... *Gatha* 1282.

Preface
xiii easy way... *Gatha* 2458.
xiii business that will profit... *Gatha* 101.

PART ONE: LIFE AND TEACHINGS

Introduction
4   They gave to India the concept... *The Divine Name in the Indian Tradition,* p.215.
4   a religious way of life based... *The Saint-Poets of Maharashtra,* p.158.
5   Prof. K.V. Belsare explains that Indian culture... *Tukaram,* p.1.
5   Indulge not the body in sense pleasures... *Gatha* 660.
6   A saint, in short, is God on earth... *Tukaram,* p.2.
6   Tukaram has been acclaimed as the greatest... *Psalms of Maratha Saints,* p.18.

Life Sketch

Early life

9   Deeply grieved am I... *Gatha* 1333.
9   I am harassed to the extreme... *Gatha* 914.
9   Loss of health or wealth... *Tukaram,* p.12.
10 His suffering made him poignantly aware... *Tukaram,* p.13.
10 The body and riches are a mirage... *Gatha* 1421.
10 There is no peace on this earth... *Gatha* 73.
11 My wife is dead, she is freed from suffering... *Gatha* 778.
11 Let me not desire anything, O Tuka... *Gatha* 1207.

Search for a saint

12 Life's mission will be fulfilled... *Gatha* 2006.
12 The sun, the lamp and the diamond... *Gatha* 1260.
12 words are like nectar... *Gatha* 1550.
12 If your heart merges in the heart of a saint... *Gatha* 1195.
12 Tukaram asks the Lord to keep him... *Gatha* 4109.
12 Even if he could not find God... *Gatha* 1076.
13 I wish to do ceaseless repetition... *Gatha* 4014.
13 He did not move his body even slightly... *Gatha* 4354.
13 When my neck feels a jerk... *Life of Tukaram,* p.132.

Initiation, spiritual practice and longing

13 I am weary even of my own family... *Gatha* 3406.
14 I crave neither heaven... *Gatha* 4156.
14 When will I be lucky enough to see... *Gatha* 2468.
15 Let my throat cry for you... *Gatha* 2423.
15 How often must I tell you... *Gatha* 996.
16 A cow may be grazing in the forest... *Gatha* 1556.
16 As the lover is dear to the beloved... *Gatha* 942.
16 Who cares for heaven... *Gatha* 2915.
16 Give me only your Name... *Gatha* 3.
16 What does the lotus know... *Gatha* 533.
17 My sins stand between you and me... *Gatha* 2177.
17 I am a sinner, but it is your duty... *Gatha* 1825.
17 I am a sinner, but I am your marked soul... *Gatha* 1055.
17 get entangled in the great trap... *Gatha* 2808.
17 What shall I do with this mind... *Gatha* 4053.

18 I do not want to mix with people... *Gatha* 2205.
18 Please ensure that I do not like people... *Gatha* 2291.
18 I am the fallen one... *Gatha* 476.

The dark night of the soul
18 I have no strength... *Gatha* 4285.
19 My meditation is so weak... *Gatha* 1013.
19 Let me concentrate like a young girl... *Gatha* 2873.
19 I do not want honour and riches... *Gatha* 1763.
20 I long to be united with you... *Gatha* 1920.
20 I never cared for the opinion... *Gatha* 1333.
20 He was even prepared to sacrifice... *Gatha* 371.
21 O my Lord, I cannot be patient... *Gatha* 852.
21 I am dying to see your form... *Gatha* 3037.
21 As a chakor bird waits... *Gatha* 2821.
21 I am suffering so much in my desire... *Gatha* 3418.
21 O breath of my life, please remove... *Gatha* 3785.
21 Why don't you have pity on me... *Gatha* 543.
22 My endeavours have come to naught... *Gatha* 1737.
22 I see God's face... *Gatha* 2019.
22 pilgrimage to God is an ascent... *Tukaram*, p.16
23 O my Lord, let my eyes be forever... *Gatha* 3.
23 Dr S. D. Pendse commented... *Sakshatkari Sant Tukaram*, p.20.
23 Pray, heed my last prayer... *Gatha* 4405.
24 My tongue has gone crazy... *Gatha* 3079.
24 In my mouth let there be only... *Gatha* 3042.

God-realization
24 After fifteen days I saw the divinity... *Gatha* 4354.
24 I have merged fully into the incomparable One... *Gatha* 4326.
25 The sun and its rays cannot be separated... *Gatha* 577.
25 The lamp in my hand has dispelled... *Gatha* 2003.
25 A stream of immeasurable happiness... *Gatha* 2020.
25 Tuka has merged in the Lord... *Gatha* 4313.
26 Now my joy fills all the three worlds... *Gatha* 2669.
26 The supreme state of bliss... *Gatha* 4330.
26 God is the giver and God is the enjoyer... *Gatha* 321.
26 The outer world has no attraction... *Gatha* 1637.

27 I did service to the Lord without looking... *Gatha* 2433.
27 The Lord has placed the treasure... *Gatha* 2546.
27 The impossible is made possible... *Gatha* 298.

Tukaram's mission
27 I have been smaller than an atom... *Gatha* 993.
27 God is my constant companion... *Tukaram,* p.33.

Tukaram's hurdles and his persecution
30 Tukaram's first offence was to write... *Says Tuka,* p.viii.
31 I am going to my home town and... *Gatha* 4471.

Tukaram as a person
32 Make me small and humble, O Lord... *Gatha* 1282.
33 To me, wealth is like cow's meat... *Gatha* 1893.
33 Tukaram's asceticism may be misunderstood... *Life of Tukaram,* p.vii.
34 This incident is reminiscent of... *Swakashtachi Kamai* (*Honest Living* in Marathi), (Beas, Punjab: Radha Soami Satsang Beas, 1998), p.14.

Tukaram's poems
35 If you say that I am composing... *Gatha* 1007.
35 Soami Ji Maharaj says the same... *Sar Bachan Radha Soami Chhanda Band,* Seth Shiv Dayal Singh (Beas, Punjab:Radha Soami Satsang Beas, 1989), p.94:9:9:12.

Tukaram's Teachings
36 So he has come to explain them anew... *Gatha* 520.

The significance of human birth
36 Cream, curd and butter... *Gatha* 4353.
37 The soul was in truth free... *Gatha* 1567.
37 After many years I got this fortune... *Gatha* 3048.
37 The temple of the living God... *Gatha* 660.
37 A life of devotion to the Lord... *Gatha* 254.
38 When you get a human birth... *Gatha* 2018.

Outer display, external religious practices, rituals and ceremonies
38 What have you gained by pilgrimages... *Gatha* 1732.
38 we find only water and stones... *Gatha* 114.
39 Tukaram denounces empty display... *Gatha* 810.
39 O Lord, you are supreme bliss incarnate... *Gatha* 700.

Initiation by a true Master
40 The Shabd is truly the essence... *Gatha* 426.
40 Knowledge of the Ultimate... *Gatha* 4407.
40 My Master has blessed me... *Chhandabaddha Gatha* 24.
40 By the grace of my Satguru... *Gatha* 2668.
40 The Lord has met me in the form... *Gatha* 4357.
40 Lest this human birth be wasted... *Gatha* 4380.

Qualifications and obligations of seekers
41 If you love your Master with your... *Gatha* 1195.
41 As the moth loves the flame... *Gatha* 1184.
41 It is only a person with past merits... *Gatha* 4124.

A true Master
42 If an exhausted man goes to another... *Gatha* 4061.
42 He deplores those who pose as sadhus... *Gatha* 3866.
42 Clothes do not make someone a saint... *Gatha* 2305.
42 A saint is one whose attachment... *Gatha* 366.
42 He sees God everywhere... *Gatha* 321.
42 A saint's heart is like butter... *Gatha* 347.
43 Saints come into this world... *Gatha* 1510.
43 The Lord has sent me to this world... *Gatha* 519.
43 What do I know of deep philosophy... *Gatha* 1007.
43 I have opened the treasure trove... *Gatha* 3250.

The Lord's Name or Nam
44 The Word is God; let us honour... *Gatha* 3396.
44 The Unstruck Music reverberates in all... *Gatha* 1789.
45 With the Name the wheel of births... *Gatha* 1100.
45 If one is attached to the Name... *Gatha* 3113.
45 Sitting at the Lord's feet... *Gatha* 2542.
45 The Lord has taken up residence... *Gatha* 3502.

45 What could not be understood... *Gatha* 3047.
46 In Kaliyug salvation is obtained... *Gatha* 2874.

Meditation
46 You will not be called valiant... *Gatha* 1186.
46 A root manages to find a way... *Gatha* 1400.
47 When you depend on him... *Gatha* 2659.

Simran
47 The sun rises in the midst... *Chhandabaddha Gatha* 96.
47 One who repeats the Lord's Name... *Gatha* 1096.
48 By repetition man becomes God... *Gatha* 4165.

Dhyan and darshan
48 Inner contemplation is... *Focus on Tukaram from a Fresh Angle,*
    p.10.
48 My happiness knows no bounds... *Gatha* 2019.
48 An intense longing for you forever resides... *Gatha* 1515.

Bhajan
49 In Kaliyug, listen to the Sound... *Gatha* 96.
49 When I become the Lord's slave... *Gatha* 1122.
49 The inner Light, which was veiled... *Gatha* 2847.
49 The unquenchable flame shines... *Gatha* 3502.

Dying while living
50 I have died to live... *Gatha* 537.
50 Once my body was vacated... *Gatha* 3502.

The mind
51 The first obstacle on the path... *The Divine Name in the Indian
    Tradition,* p.124.
51 Worldly happiness is like a mirage... *Gatha* 1421.
51 Merits and demerits do not depend... *Gatha* 4030.
52 Fix the mind on God... *Gatha* 3734.
52 Keep your mind in one place... *Gatha* 4304.

Negative emotions

52 Control the senses and forgive others... *Gatha* 81.
52 not to talk to a woman when alone... *Gatha* 2846.
53 O God, do not give me the company... *Gatha* 523.
53 After all, how much does a person require... *Gatha* 2016.
53 One should live in this world... *Gatha* 2967.
53 One who has purged himself of ego... *Gatha* 53.
54 Due to the Lord's Name, I have become... *Gatha* 4303.
54 I have discarded for good all thoughts... *Gatha* 2668.

Worry, laziness, sleep and overeating

54 In life there is sometimes happiness... *Gatha* 2819.
54 Face whatever comes in life... *Gatha* 2396.
54 In the bosom of the stone... *Gatha* 602.
55 With laziness and sleep... *Tukaram: Bhakticha Dangora,* p.44.
55 Do not sleep much, eat less... *Gatha* 2846.
55 What shall I do with more sweets... *Gatha* 1202.

Ethical conduct

56 If you do not desire others' money... *Gatha* 61.
56 We are obliged to these washermen... *Gatha* 1723.
56 The Lord is within every being... *Gatha* 4178.
60 God-realization is not a joke... *Gatha* 767.

Satsang and the company of devotees

60 The Lord is present at satsang... *Gatha* 2929.
60 The fires of the three attributes... *Gatha* 1260.
60 come into this world only to liberate... *Gatha* 1510.

Glossary

abhang   Literally, ceaseless and unbroken; devotional poem or verse by saints of Maharashtra.

Adi Granth   Primal *(adi)* scripture *(granth)*; also called *Sri Guru Granth Sahib;* the name given to the scripture that brings together hymns of the first five Gurus and the ninth Guru in the line of Guru Nanak as well as hymns of numerous other saints from various parts of India and neighbouring countries. The Adi Granth has become the sacred scripture of the Sikhs.

attributes   *See* **gunas**

bhajan   Worship with music and singing, devotional songs; the practice of meditation in general, or specifically listening to the inner Sound. When a disciple achieves concentration through repetition and contemplation, he is able to make contact with this inner Sound. When the soul hears the Shabd, the source from which it has long been separated, it is irresistibly attracted by its sweet melody and begins to rise with it to planes of higher consciousness. This practice is also called Surat Shabd Yoga.

bhakti   Devotion, worship, adoration; a spiritual discipline undertaken to please God, a deity or other revered being. Guru bhakti is devotion to the Guru—following a path of spiritual discipline in accordance with the Guru's instructions.

Brahma   The god of creation in the Hindu triad: Brahma the creator, Vishnu the sustainer and Shiva the destroyer.

brahmin   The priestly class; the first and the highest of the four castes into which Hindu society was divided, the other

164

three being *kshatriya*—the regal and warrior class; *vaishya*—trading and agricultural class; *shudra*—menial and unskilled labour class.

cycle of birth and death   The endless round of transmigration, in which the soul incarnates and reincarnates in different life forms according to the consequences of karma. The soul moves from one life form to another, reaping the harvest of seeds it has sown in previous lives. *See also* **karma, wheel of eighty-four**

darshan   Sight, vision, seeing, having a glimpse of someone; looking at someone or something with admiration, love and reverence; looking at the Master or an image of a deity with such absorption that we forget everything else, even our own body, and lose the sense of our separate existence. The darshan that the mystics generally talk about, however, and the one that elevates the soul to spheres of higher consciousness, is inner darshan, the darshan of the Radiant Form of the Master. This darshan is attained through a process of deep inner contemplation.

dhyan   Attention, concentration, contemplation; the second aspect of the spiritual practice taught by the saints, in which the disciple contemplates on the form of his Master so as to hold the mind still at the eye centre. True contemplation is achieved naturally once the attention is focused and the mind becomes fully concentrated. *See also* **simran**

Dnyaneshwar (1275–1296)   Dnyaneshwar is credited with laying the foundation of the bhakti movement in Maharashtra. He wrote a commentary on the *Bhagavad Gita* known as *Dnyaneshwari,* which is recognized as authoritative and is greatly revered in Maharashtra.

Eknath (1533–1569)   A famous Maharashtrian saint and poet who advocated mystic devotion, Eknath wrote several narrative pieces and abhangs that expressed his mystical experience. His commentary on the eleventh chapter of *Bhagavata Purana* has become a classic in Maharashtra.

feet of the Master or Lord On the human level, the feet of the Master symbolize shelter or protection for the disciple, and surrender at the Master's feet expresses humility and submission. Out of respect, a Master's feet are referred to as lotus feet. The lotus feet of the Master can also have an esoteric significance, referring to the feet of the Radiant Form of the Master seen within at the eight-petalled lotus on the astral plane. Drinking the nectar flowing from the Master's feet or bathing in the misty light or dust of those feet are spontaneous expressions of love for the Master. Similarly, clinging to the feet of the Lord or laying one's heart at his feet can signify meeting the Lord, who is one with the Master, within.

gatha Collection; specifically a collection of abhangs (devotional poems) by saints from Maharashtra. *See also* **abhang**

gunas Attributes, qualities or states in nature. The operation of the world is made possible by the interplay of three gunas: 1) satogun, the quality of goodness, peace, beauty, rhythm and harmony; 2) rajogun, the quality of action, achievement, passion and pride; and 3) tamogun, the quality of darkness, inertia and ignorance. All the three gunas are present in human nature, varying in degree according to individuals, and each can be enhanced by providing conditions conducive to its growth and development. The predominance (permanent or temporary) of a particular guna in human nature creates corresponding tendencies in behaviour.

Indra According to Hindu scriptures, Indra is the ruler of paradise or the heavens.

Kabir (1398?–1518) One of the best-known saints of India, he lived a century before Tukaram. Part of his writings were incorporated into the Adi Granth in 1604. His writings are still widely quoted in daily life throughout India and have been incorporated into folk music and culture. Legend surrounds his birth and background, and both Hindus and Muslims claim him as theirs. He travelled extensively and taught the practice of the Word, speaking out against external forms of worship and all institutionalized centres of power that keep people from the truth.

Kal Literally, time or death; the ruler of the three worlds who administers justice strictly according to the law of karma. Also known as Brahm, the universal mind. The domain of Kal is the whole creation up to Trikuti, which includes the physical, astral and causal worlds and is destroyed at the time of dissolution. *See also* **Trikuti, three worlds**

Kaliyug The fourth cycle of time, known as the Dark Age or the Iron Age, the present era, an age in which the light of truth is heavily veiled. According to Hindu scriptures, time is divided into four yugas or cycles: 1) Satyug or Kritayug, the Age of Truth or the Golden Age; 2) Tretayug, the Silver Age; 3) Dwaparyug, the Copper or Bronze Age; and 4) Kaliyug, the Dark or Iron Age.

karma Action; the law of action and reaction, cause and effect, whereby the soul has to face the consequences of all its actions. It is the law of karma that keeps the soul imprisoned in the creation, as it has to continue taking birth in different life forms to account for its actions in previous lives. *See also* **cycle of birth and death**

kirtan Singing the praise of God. Tukaram uses the term for singing the praise of God vocally, with or without accompaniment of musical instruments, and for the divine music heard within by spiritual practitioners.

lotus feet *See* **feet of the Master**

Maharashtra Presently a state in western India; the region of western India where Tukaram lived.

maya Illusion that has the appearance of reality; the entire creation; the three worlds (physical, astral and causal) ruled by Brahm. Maya denotes anything that comes and goes; it is often described as the web of illusion, referring to the transience of the creation.

Nam Name *(naam);* Nam represents not only the dynamic power of God that created and sustains the universe, but also the current that can unite souls with God. In order to elevate human consciousness, which normally operates at the gross level of mind and senses, Nam functions at two levels: at the human level as the initiation mantra granted by a true Master, and at God's level as the divine melody called Shabd, experienced through soul consciousness. It must be emphasized that the Nam mantra is invested with the potential to reveal the Shabd of the highest stage only when it is granted by a living true Master. *See also* **Shabd**

Namdev (1270–1350) A Maharashtrian saint who was a tailor and calico printer by profession, Namdev first had his headquarters at Pandharpur in Maharashtra. Later he moved to North India, and he passed away in Punjab. He wrote thousands of devotional poems in Hindi, Marathi and Punjabi. His writings are preserved in *Namdev Gatha,* and some poems are included in the Adi Granth.

Name *See* Nam

Parbrahm Beyond Brahm; the third inner region beyond the realms ruled by Brahm.

pralabdh karma (prarabdh karma) Fate karma; our destiny in this life, created by actions in past lives, upon which the present life is based. *See also* **karma**

Puranas Literally, the ancient ones; religio-mythological stories written in Sanskrit. There are eighteen principal Puranas, written at different times. They contain myths about the lives and deeds of the gods, sages and kings, and discuss the creation, destruction and renewal of the universe.

satguru   True *(sat)* spiritual teacher *(guru)*; a Master who has access to Sach Khand, the fifth spiritual region. In this book, a Satguru refers to a saint who is ordained to take certain allotted souls back to God by initiating them into the yoga of Shabd.

satsang   Association *(sang)* with the true *(sat)*; the company of saints or advanced souls. The term 'satsang' is commonly used to denote a spiritual discourse or a gathering of devotees held under the auspices of a Master. Inner satsang, the highest form of satsang, is the conscious encounter of the soul with the Word (truth) on the inner planes of being.

Shabd   Sound, voice, word, hymn; esoterically, the underlying current of divine energy that created and sustains the universe, also called Word, Logos, Name, Holy Spirit, sound current, unstruck music, music of the spheres, and so forth. It was through Shabd, the eternal power of God, that souls were sent down from their original home to inhabit the creation, and it is through the same power that they must retrace their journey homewards. However, no one but a true living Master can reveal the secret of Shabd and connect the disciple's consciousness to it. *See also* **Nam**

simran   Remembrance, repetition of a mantra, calling to mind or meditating upon the Supreme Being. Simran is the first part of the spiritual practice as taught by the saints. Through simran the attention is withdrawn from the outer world and concentrated at the eye centre.

Soham (Sohang)   Literally, 'I am He'; the stage where the soul realizes its identity with God, recognizing that it is of the same essence as the Lord, but is, as yet, separate from him. This occurs at the threshold of the eternal region, Sach Khand, where the soul will merge into oneness with the Lord.

third eye A point in the subtle body between and behind the two eyebrows. The third eye is the seat of the mind and the soul in the human body and the point at which practitioners of meditation concentrate their attention in order to withdraw the soul currents from the physical body and enter the inner realms. Also referred to as the tenth door, the gateway to liberation, the eye centre.

three worlds The physical world, the more subtle astral world, and the even finer causal world, where pure mind is dominant. *See also* **Trikuti, Kal**

Trikuti The headquarters of the causal plane and the seat of universal mind or Brahm, who is the ruler of the three worlds—physical, astral and causal. Trikuti is the second stage on the inner journey described by the Saints.

Vedas Literally, knowledge; revealed knowledge as embodied in the four early Hindu scriptures written in Sanskrit *(Rig Veda, Sam Veda, Yajur Veda, Atharva Veda)*. Also refers to Vedic literature in general, including the Upanishads and various interpretative texts.

wheel of birth and death *See* **cycle of birth and death**

wheel of eighty-four The wheel of eighty-four *(chaurasi)* refers to the eighty-four lakh (8,400,000) life forms that according to Indian tradition make up the manifest creation. It is described as a cycle, a circle or a wheel—an endless round of birth and death—due to the law of karma, whereby all life forms have to undergo the consequences of their own actions. The soul moves from one form to another, reaping the harvest of seeds it has sown in previous lives. Saints describe the soul's pain by speaking of *chaurasi* as a prison, an entangling web, a vast net, the fearful ocean of existence. *See also* **karma**

Word *See* **Shabd**

Bibliography

English

Abbot, Justin E. *Life of Tukaram*. Delhi: Motilal Banarsidass, 1980.

Belsare, K.V. *Tukaram*. Mumbai: Government of Maharashtra, 1985.

Chitre, Dilip. *Says Tuka*. Pune: Penguin Books, 1991.

Fraser, J. Nelson and K. B.Marathe. *The Poems of Tukarama*. Delhi: Motilal Banarsidass, 1981.

Macnicol, Nicol. *Psalms of Maratha Saints*. Bombay: Oxford University Press, 1919.

Ranade, R. D. *Mysticism in Maharashtra*. Delhi: Motilal Banarsidass, 1988.

Sardar, G. B. *The Saint-Poets of Maharashtra*. Bombay: Orient Longmans, 1969.

Sharma, S. R. *Focus on Tukaram from a Fresh Angle*. Bombay: Popular Book Depot, 1962.

———. *Tukaram's Teachings*. Bombay: Bharatiya Vidya Bhavan, 1964.

Tulpule, S. G. *The Divine Name in the Indian Tradition*. New Delhi: Indus Publishing Co., 1991.

Marathi

Belsare, K.V. *Bhagvantachya Namache Divya Sangeet*. Mumbai: Tridal Prakashan, 1997.

———. *Shri Tukaramanchi Nam Sadhana.* Mumbai: Tridal Prakashan, 1997.

Bhave, V. L. and S.G. Tulpule. *Maharashtra Saraswat*. Pune: V.G. Mate 'Vishwakarma', 1976.

Das, Babaji. *Vishwa Sant Shri Tukaram Maharajanche Sadeha Vaikunth Gaman.* Mumbai: S. B. Chavan & B.S. Vare, 1978.

Nirantar, G. B. *Marathi Vangmayacha Paramarsh.* Pune: Venus Publications, 1957.

Pendse, S. D. *Sakshatkari Sant Tukaram.* Pune: Continental Prakashan, 1972.

Ranade, R. D. *Tukaram Vachanamrit.* Pune: V.V. Apte, 1991.

Tukaram. *Sartha Shri Tukaramachi Gatha.* Edited by Vishnubuva Jog. Mumbai: Keshav Bhikaji Dhavle, 1999 (referred to in this book as *Jog Gatha*).

———. *Sartha Tukaram Gatha.* 3 vols. Edited by P. N. Joshi. Mumbai: Shri Bharat Book Depot, 1968 (referred to in this book as *Gatha*).

———. *Shri Tukaram Bavanchya Abhanganchi Gatha.* Edited by Vishnu Parshuram Shastri Pandit. Vol. 2. Mumbai: Indu Prakash Press, 1950.

———. *Shri Tukaram Maharaj Yanchya Abhanganchi Chhandabaddha Gatha.* Edited by R. K. Dhongde. Satara: Sant Seva Prakashan, 1965 (referred to in this book as *Chhandabaddha Gatha*).

———. *Shri Tukarambavanchya Abhanganchi Gatha.* Edited by P. M. Lad. Pune: Government of Maharashtra, 1991.

Tulpule, G.V. *Sakshatkar Pathavar Tukaram.* Sangli: G.V. Tulpule, 1954.

———. *Tukaram: Bhakticha Dangora.* Sangli: Shri Ganpati Sansthan Press, 1972.

Index of Marathi First Lines

173

Subject Index

Addresses for Information
and Books

INDIAN SUB-CONTINENT

INDIA
The Secretary
Radha Soami Satsang Beas
P.O. Dera Baba Jaimal Singh 143204
District Amritsar, Punjab

NEPAL
Mr. Dal Bahadur Shreshta
Radha Soami Satsang Beas
P. O. Box 1646, Gongabu, Dhapasi,
Kathmandu

PAKISTAN
Dr. Bhagwandas M. Pathai
Resham Gali, Larkana, Sindh

SRI LANKA
Mr. D. H. Jiwat
c/o Geekay Ltd.
33 Bankshall Street, Colombo 11

SOUTHEAST ASIA

*Representative for other countries
of Far-East Asia:*

Mrs. Cami Moss
Radha Soami Satsang Beas, Hostel 6
P.O. Dera Baba Jaimal Singh 143204
District Amritsar, Punjab, India

MALAYSIA
Mr. Selvarajoo Pragasam
No. 15 Jalan SL 10/4,
Bandar Sg. Long,
43000 Kajang

THAILAND
Mr. Harmahinder Singh Sethi
58/32 Rachdapitsek Road, Soi 16
Thapra, Bangkok Yai 10600

INDONESIA
Mr. Ramesh Sadarangani
Jalan Pasir Putih IV/16, Block F 4
Ancol Timur, Jakarta Utara 14430

PHILIPPINES
Mr. Kay Sham
Radha Soami Satsang Beas
#1268 General Luna Street
Paco, Manila

SINGAPORE
Mrs. Asha Melwani
Radha Soami Satsang Beas
19 Amber Road, Singapore 439868

ASIA PACIFIC

AUSTRALIA
Mr. Pradeep Raniga
P.O. Box 642
Balwyn North, Victoria 3104

183

NEW ZEALAND
Mr. Tony Waddicor
Science of the Soul Study Centre
P. O. Box 5331
Auckland

GUAM
Mrs. Hoori M. Sadhwani
115 Alupang Cove
241 Condo Lane, Tamuning 96911

HONG KONG
Mr. Manoj Sabnani
T.S.T., P.O. Box 90745
Kowloon

JAPAN
Mr. Jani G. Mohinani
Radha Soami Satsang Beas
1-2-18 Nakajimadori
Aotani, Chuo-Ku
Kobe 651-0052

SOUTH KOREA
Dr. Moon Jin Hee
#2011 Jung San 4RI Buron-Myun
Won Ju-City
Kang Won Do
Korea 220-814

TAIWAN, R.O.C.
Mr. Larry Teckchand Nanwani
P. O. Box 68-1414
Taipei

NORTH AMERICA

CANADA
Mr. John Abel
#701-1012 Beach Avenue
Vancouver, B.C. V6E 1T7

Mrs. Meena Khanna
149 Elton Park Road
Oakville, Ontario L6J 4C2

UNITED STATES
Dr. Vincent P. Savarese
3507 Saint Elizabeth Road
Glendale, CA 91206-1227

Science of the Soul Study Center
2415 East Washington Street
Petaluma, CA 94954

Dr. Frank E. Vogel
71 Old Farm Road
Concord, MA 01742

Science of the Soul Study Center
4115 Gillespie Street
Fayetteville, NC 28306-9053

Dr. John Templer
114 Verdier Road
Beaufort, SC 29902-5440

Dr. Eugene Ivash
4701 Shadow Lane
Austin, TX 78731-5334

CARIBBEAN

*Representative for the Caribbean,
Suriname and Guyana:*
Mr. Sean Finnigan
P. O. Box 2314
Port-au-Prince
Haiti, W. I.

BARBADOS
Mr. Deepak Nebhani
Radha Soami Satsang Beas
Lot No. 10, 5ᵗʰ Avenue
Belleville, St. Michael
Barbados, W. I.

CURACAO
Mrs. Komal Lachman Vasandani
P. O. Box 426
Curacao, N. A.

GUYANA
Mrs. Rajni B. Manglani
A-80 Eping Avenue,
Bel Air Park,
Georgetown, Guyana

JAMAICA
Mrs. Shammi Khiani
P. O. Box 22
Montego Bay
Jamaica, W. I.

ST. MAARTEN
Mrs. Kanchan Mahbubani
R.S.S.B. Foundation
P. O. Box 978
Phillipsburg
St. Maarten, N. A.

SURINAME
Mr. Chandru Samtani
15 Venus Straat
Paramaribo
Suriname

TRINIDAD
Mrs. Anganie Chatlani
8A Saddle Road, Maraval
Trinidad, W. I.

CENTRAL AMERICA

BELIZE
Mrs. Chand Babani
5789 Goldson Avenue, Belize City

MEXICO
Mr. Jorge Angel Santana
Jacarandas #30
FTO. Azaleas Recidencial
Zapopan 45090

PANAMA
Mr. Deepak Dhanani
Altos Del Bosque
Residencial El Doral, Casa 195
Repubica De Panama

SOUTH AMERICA

Representative for other countries of South America (Argentina, Brazil, Chile):

Mr. Hiro W. Balani
P.O. Box 486,
Malaga 29012, Spain

COLOMBIA
Mrs. Emma Orozco
P. O. Box 49744, Medellin

ECUADOR
Dr. Fernando Flores Villalva
Calle de la Grulla, lote 11
Urbanizacion Valle 3 - Cumbaya
Quito

PERU
Mrs. Haseen Mirpuri
Av. Benavides 120-901, Peru
Miraflores, Lima

185

VENEZUELA
Radha Soami Satsang Beas
Avenida Las Samanes
c/c Calle Los Naranjos
Conjunto Florida 335, Urb. La Florida
Caracas

EUROPE

AUSTRIA
Mr. Hansjorg Hammerer
Sezenweingasse 10, Salzburg A-5020

BELGIUM
Mr. Piet J. E. Vosters
Lindekensstraat 39 Box 4
Turnhout 2300

BULGARIA
Mr. Emilio Saev
Foundation Radha Soami Satsang Beas
Bulgaria
P. O. Box 39, 8000 Bourgas

CYPRUS
Mr. Heraclis Achilleos
P. O. Box 29077, Nicosia 1035

CZECH REPUBLIC
Mr. Vladimir Skalsky
Maratkova 916,
142 00 Prague 412

DENMARK
Mr. Tony Sharma
Sven Dalsgaardsvej 33
DK-7430 Ikast

FINLAND
Ms. Ritta Anneli Wingfield
Hansinkatu 12 C 33
01400 Vantaa near Helsinki

FRANCE
Ct. Pierre de Proyart
7 Quai Voltaire, Paris 75007

GERMANY
Mr. Rudolf Walberg
P. O. Box 1544
D-65800 Bad Soden / Taunus

GIBRALTAR
Mr. Sunder Mahtani
Radha Soami Satsang Beas
Flat 401 Ocean Heights, 4th Floor
Queensway

GREECE
Mrs. Eleftheria Tsolaki
P.O. Box 35
Paleo Faliro 17503, Athens

ITALY
Mrs. Wilma Salvatori Torri
Via Bacchiglione 3, 00199 Rome

THE NETHERLANDS
(HOLLAND)
Radha Soami Satsang Beas - Nederland
Middenweg 145 E
1394 AH Nederhorst den Berg

NORWAY
Mr. Sohan Singh Mercy
St. Halvardsgt. 6
N-3015 Drammen

POLAND
Mr. Vinod Sharma
UL. 1go Sierpien 36 B M-100
PL-02-134, Warsaw

PORTUGAL
Mrs. Sharda Lodhia
Rua Quinta Das Palmeiras, Lote 68
11° andar C, Oeiras 2780-145

ROMANIA
Mrs. Carmen Cismas
C.P. 6-12
Braila-810474

SLOVENIA
Mr. Marko Bedina
Brezje pri Trzicu 68
4290 Trzic

SPAIN
Mr. J. W. Balani
Calle Panorama no. 15
Cerrado de Calderon
Malaga 29018

SWEDEN
Mr. Lennart Zachen
Norra Sonnarpsvägen 29
S-286 72 Asljunga

SWITZERLAND
Mr. Sebastian Zust Bischof
Weissenrainstrasse 48
CH 8707 Uetikon am See (ZH)

UNITED KINGDOM
Mr. Narinder Singh Johal
Haynes Park Estate
Haynes, Bedford MK45 3BL

AFRICA

BENIN
Mr. Jaikumar T. Vaswani
01 Boite Postale 951,
Recette Principale, Cotonou

BOTSWANA
Dr. Krishan Lal Bhateja
P. O. Box 402539, Gaborone

GHANA
Mr. Murli Chatani
Radha Soami Satsang Beas
P. O. Box 3976, Accra

IVORY COAST
Mr. Konan N'Dri
08 Boite Postale 569
Abidjan 08

KENYA
Mr. Surinder Singh Ghir
P. O. Box 15134,
Langata 00509, Nairobi

LESOTHO
Mr. Sello Wilson Moseme
P. O. Box 750
Leribe 300

LIBYA (G.S.P.L.A.J.)
Mr. Roshan Lal
P.O. Box 38930
Bani Walid

MAURITIUS
Mrs. Doolaree Nuckcheddy
17 Avenue Le Conte De Lisle
Quatre Bornes

NAMIBIA
Mrs. Jennifer Mary Carvill
P. O. Box 1258
Swakopmund 9000

NIGERIA
Mr. Nanik N. Balani
P.O. Box 10407, Lagos

RÉUNION
Ms. Danielle Hoareau
23 Rue Juiliette Dodu
97400 St. Denis

SIERRA LEONE
Mr. Kishore S. Mahboobani
P. O. Box 369
Freetown

SOUTH AFRICA
Radha Soami Satsang Beas
14-16 Hope Street
Gardens Cape Town
Waterfront 8002

Mr. Gordon Clive Wilson
P. O. Box 47182, Greyville 4023

Mr. Sam Busa
P. O. Box 41355, Craighall 2024

SWAZILAND
Mr. Peter Dunseith
P. O. Box 423, Mbabane

TANZANIA
Mr. Surinder Singh Oshan
P.O. Box 6984, Dar-Es-Salaam

UGANDA
Mr. Sylvester Kakooza
Radha Soami Satsang Beas
P. O. Box 31381, Kampala

ZAMBIA
Mr. Chrispin Lwali
P. O. Box 12094
Nchanga, North Township
Chingola, Lusaka

ZIMBABWE
Mrs. Dorothy Roodt
P. O. Box 7095, Harare

MIDDLE EAST

BAHRAIN
Mr. Mangat Rai Rudra
Flat No. 12 Building No. 1694
Road No. 627, Block 306
Manama

ISRAEL
Mr. Michael Yaniv
Moshav Sde Nitzan 59, I1
D.N. Hanegev 85470

KUWAIT
Mr. Vijay Kumar
P. O. Box 1913
13020 Safat

U.A.E.
Mr. Mohanlal Badlani
R.S.S.B. P.O. Box 37816
Dubai

Books on This Science

SOAMI JI MAHARAJ
Sar Bachan Prose
Sar Bachan Poetry (Selections)

BABA JAIMAL SINGH
Spiritual Letters (to Hazur Maharaj Sawan Singh: 1896-1903)

MAHARAJ SAWAN SINGH
The Dawn of Light (letters to Western disciples: 1911-1934)
Discourses on Sant Mat
My Submission (introduction to Philosophy of the Masters)
Philosophy of the Masters (Gurmat Sidhant), in 5 volumes
    (an encyclopedia on the teachings of the Saints)
Spiritual Gems (letters to Western disciples: 1919-1948)
Tales of the Mystic East (as narrated in satsangs)

MAHARAJ JAGAT SINGH
The Science of the Soul (discourses and letters: 1948-1951)

MAHARAJ CHARAN SINGH
Die to Live (answers to questions on meditation)
Divine Light (discourses and letters: 1959-1964)
Light on Saint John
Light on Saint Matthew
Light on Sant Mat (discourses and letters: 1952-1958)
The Master Answers (to audiences in America: 1964)
The Path (first part of Divine Light)
Quest for Light (letters: 1965-1971)
Spiritual Discourses, in 2 volumes
Spiritual Heritage (from tape-recorded talks)
Thus Saith the Master (to audiences in America: 1970)

BOOKS ABOUT THE MASTERS
Call of the Great Master—Diwan Daryai Lal Kapur
Heaven on Earth—Diwan Daryai Lal Kapur
Treasure Beyond Measure—Shanti Sethi
With a Great Master in India—Julian P. Johnson
With the Three Masters, in 2 volumes—from the diary of
    Rai Sahib Munshi Ram

189

BOOKS ON THIS SCIENCE

INTRODUCTION TO SPIRITUALITY
A Spiritual Primer—Hector Esponda Dubin
Honest Living: A Means to an End—M. F. Singh
The Inner Voice—Colonel C. W. Sanders
Liberation of the Soul—J. Stanley White
Life is Fair: The Law of Cause and Effect—Brian Hines

BOOKS ON MYSTICISM
A Treasury of Mystic Terms, Part I: The Principles of Mysticism
(6 volumes)—John Davidson
The Holy Name: Mysticism in Judaism—Miriam Caravella
Yoga and the Bible—Joseph Leeming

BOOKS ON SANT MAT IN GENERAL
In Search of the Way—Flora E. Wood
Living Meditation: A Journey beyond Body and Mind
—Hector Esponda Dubin
Message Divine—Shanti Sethi
The Mystic Philosophy of Sant Mat—Peter Fripp
Mysticism, The Spiritual Path, in 2 volumes—Lekh Raj Puri
The Path of the Masters—Julian P. Johnson
Radha Soami Teachings—Lekh Raj Puri
A Soul's Safari—Netta Pfeifer

MYSTICS OF THE EAST SERIES
Bulleh Shah—J. R. Puri and T.R. Shangari
Dadu, The Compassionate Mystic—K. N. Upadhyaya
Dariya Sahib, Saint of Bihar—K. N. Upadhyaya
Guru Nanak, His Mystic Teachings—J. R. Puri
Guru Ravidas, Life and Teachings—K. N. Upadhyaya
Kabir, The Great Mystic—Isaac A. Ezekiel
Kabir, The Weaver of God's Name—V. K. Sethi
Mira, The Divine Lover—V. K. Sethi
Saint Namdev—J. R. Puri and V. K. Sethi
Saint Paltu—Isaac A. Ezekiel
Sarmad, Jewish Saint of India—Isaac A. Ezekiel
Sultan Bahu—J. R. Puri and K. S. Khak
Tukaram, The Ceaseless Song of Devotion—C. Rajwade
Tulsi Sahib, Saint of Hathras—J. R. Puri and V. K. Sethi